Wakefield Press

Mezze to Milk Tart

Cecile Yazbek was born into a Lebanese family in South Africa and studied social sciences at Rhodes University in Grahamstown. She was a voluntary community worker in Cape Town and migrated to Sydney in 1986 with her young family. While running Cecile's Vegetarian Kitchen, a cooking school and catering service, she worked as a volunteer coordinator at Mercy Family Centre, Sydney. She has now retired to write, read, garden and cook, not always in that order.

By the same author

Olive Trees Around my Table: Growing up Lebanese in the old South Africa

Mezze to Milk Tart

From the Middle East to Africa
in my vegetarian kitchen

Cecile Yazbek

Wakefield
Press

Wakefield Press
1 The Parade West
Kent Town
South Australia 5067
www.wakefieldpress.com.au

First published 2011

Designed by Belinda Stachowiak
Typeset by Clinton Ellicott, Wakefield Press
Printed in China through Red Planet Print Management

National Library of Australia Cataloguing-in-Publication entry

Author:	Yazbek, Cecile (Cecile Isobel), 1953– .
Title:	Mezze to milk tart: from the Middle East to Africa in my vegetarian kitchen / Cecile Yazbek.
ISBN:	978 1 86254 921 0 (pbk.).
Subjects:	Vegetarian cooking.
Dewey Number:	641.5636

For my children

Food is once again getting the respect it deserves. More than just a means of filling our bellies, eating is a way of nourishing our bodies and enriching our souls. Good food allows us to connect with the people and places where we live in the most intimate of ways – through taste.

The backlash against the insanity of industrial food has been nothing short of astonishing. The momentum of the Slow Food Movement has grown much wider than perhaps ever imagined, with more and more people realising that eating is one of life's great pleasures and that it must be more than simply topping up our stomachs at the petrol station. It is something to be savoured and something to be shared.

It's no surprise that the increased interest and popularity in real food is followed closely by gardening as people also yearn to connect with where their produce has come from. For the same reason, people are turning to farmers' markets instead of supermarkets and are choosing to buy organic and locally grown produce. The result is not only better-quality food, but there are environmental benefits too as our consumer choices favour reduced food miles, packaging and chemical use.

Three of my favourite things – gardening, eating and spending time with family and friends – are activities that can all be brought together around a dinner table. These things are intimately intertwined and one intrinsically follows the other. I must confess that it's the gardening that I'm really addicted to. It's more than just a hobby, it's also my main source of exercise and stress relief. Being a keen food gardener, there's always plenty of surplus produce, so it make sense that we share it, either by giving it away or by inviting others to join us for meals. The result is the same – relationships strengthened by good food.

And this is exactly what *Mezze to Milk Tart* is all about – enjoying simple pleasures, respecting our environment and learning from others to enrich our lives and the lives of those around us. The best way to describe this book is like sitting at a table sharing a magnificent long lunch with close friends. It's an intermingled combination of delicious recipes, fascinating stories and personal insights shared with generosity and love. Enjoy …

Josh Byrne
Organic gardener and food lover

Introduction

Vegetarianism is part of many cultures: Hinduism immediately springs to mind. Among Orthodox Christians of the Middle East as far as Iraq, Lent is a forty-day period of fasting when only one light meal is eaten per day, and they abstain from animal products. During this time the food is prepared *b'zeit* – with oil instead of the usual *samneh* (ghee, or rendered butter). It is a classically healthy vegan diet based on nuts, legumes and pulses. In Greece, the expression *sarakostiyana* expresses the absence of animal products in meals served during Lent in Greek Orthodox households. Similarly, the Copts in Egypt eat vegan-style during Lent.

In my cooking school, Cecile's Vegetarian Kitchen, the recipes I taught drew on my Lebanese heritage, southern Europe and the Mediterranean as well as the Indian cooking of my childhood. These were augmented by classes I myself attended. I reduced fats and oils and shortened methods to keep the more traditional recipes alive. We used spices that begin mildly at the Lebanese coast and crescendo in India. So the cooking that I taught was not simple beans and peas: we discovered the history and cultures of many different places – a foreign country in my kitchen. Feeding growing children, I explored the foods we ate – how and where they were produced and transported – and I became convinced that food produced unethically and through suffering would make us ill. Most of my students will say that I never tried to practise an exact science. As Granny so often told me, if you put good ingredients together, you will have a good result.

It all really began when I was a small child – lovingly nurtured by my grandmother and mother, both excellent cooks, expanded by a code of social justice I learnt at home. Combining these elements of my life, I have enjoyed bringing a broad range of people together – people who might never have met, had we not initially shared a common interest in food.

Food is a great part of the nostalgia we share. It anoints our social occasions and takes our memories to families and friends long gone. For years while the cooking school was running, and now that I have retired from teaching, I have mailed, dictated over the phone and emailed recipes to all corners of the globe, especially to former students, diners at my table and those with whom I have shared seductive food conversations. Now that those favourite recipes are gathered in this collection, I invite you to come and find your own comfort food in this exciting world where Africa meets the Mediterranean in Australia.

Welcome to my table.

May we continue to share our joy and our food, always mindful in thought and action of those who lack the bare means of survival.

'Yia sta xeria sou' (Bless your hands)

– Greek

Cecile's Vegetarian Kitchen came into being out of my desire to show interested people that vegetarian eating was more than just toast and cheese or lentil soup. As a result, many different people joined these eclectic sessions. The characters and their stories stayed in my mind. Like the young woman who asked me if I was really a vegetarian because I was the first 'fat' one she'd seen. Or the teenager who was pierced in every visible (and there was a lot on show) part: she had to stay away from the stove, as her metal bits heated up and could have branded her. And there were always a few men in the class, usually the minority: one day, a solitary man suddenly requested his classmates to apply their feminine wisdom and personal experience to his wife's intimate gynaecological problem.

I sometimes also made inappropriate comments, like the time I slopped tomato sauce over the table as I was serving a man, who turned out to be a judge: 'Oh my God,' I blurted, 'now I'm going to jail.' He said to me, gently, as if trying to coax a bandit from a bolthole with kindness, 'Why are you going to jail?' I blushed and said very quickly, 'Because in South Africa one could go to prison for anything, even making a mess.'

But the prize goes to the well-dressed matron, twin-set and pearls, busy hollowing a zucchini when she said, deadpan, as if to herself, 'Would you rather be a zucchini or a piano? Fingered or stuffed?'

I wanted to guffaw but kept the group going as there was also a very religious pair in the class and we might've ended up in deep scriptural waters as an antidote.

One day a woman was describing someone else's good fortune in envious tones. Her ongoing lament about her circumstances became so irritating I dropped my knife and announced to the stunned kitchen, 'If the grass looks greener on the other side, it's because it's had more *ess haitch* dumped on it.' That day, we finished cooking in record time.

Occasionally in a class, someone with a current drama needed to vent. We all listened respectfully and at the end of such a day, I might comment: 'Nuts, seeds, pulses and purslane – all good food for a good mood. As well as caring about what we eat, we also have to pay attention to those hidden parts of our lives that can erupt from time to time. When all looks like manure, remember to plant roses!'

So in this chapter, you are invited to join a class with some conversation and tips, with recipes to follow.

A cooking class in action.

Preparation

I always told my students to break the rules: like the one about never serving a dish you make for the first time to guests. Making a dish for the first time is interesting and we concentrate on doing it well: by all means serve it to your guests; as cook, you are the only one with an idea of the result you expect; in my experience, friends are only too happy to be invited and, like myself, are always appreciative of being cooked for.

The best way to start cooking a meal, whether for family or entertaining, is to go to the market and find what is freshest and suits your budget and taste, then look for a recipe.

For these recipes I have put some of the method instruction into the ingredients list: for example, one onion sliced in rings, or two carrots, grated. I found this most useful in class, where one looked at the list, gathered the items, prepared them for use and carried out the assembly or final method in a burst of pleasure.

Measuring

In these recipes I use standard measuring utensils:

1 cup = 250 mL
1 tablespoon = 20 mL
1 dessertspoon = 7.5 mL
1 teaspoon = 5 mL

And all the bits in-between:

⅓ cup = 80 mL
½ cup = 125 mL
½ teaspoon = 2.5 mL
pinch = 1 mL or 2 mL, according to taste

For the dimensions of a baking tin or casserole dish, turn it upside down and measure the width and the length across the bottom.

Salt and Pepper Quantities

In a list of ingredients, where a quantity is specified, it is safe to use the recommended amount. Where no quantity is mentioned, follow your taste. A sprinkling or a pinch of salt, white pepper, ground black pepper or cinnamon, means just that.

When cooking your own legumes, 1 cup dried produces 2 cups cooked and requires 1 level teaspoon of salt. Consequently in recipes using salted legumes (and tins, unless specified, all have salt added), add very little, if any, to the rest of the ingredients. It is better to use salt in the cooking process rather than adding it at the table because that way one uses less overall.

Scissors and Knives

A pair of sharp, medium-size scissors is invaluable in the kitchen for cutting Lebanese and Turkish breads, and is especially useful for snipping sun-dried tomatoes.

A good selection of sharp knives is handy: small parer, medium slicer and large chopper. Although one is not slicing into flesh, a sharp knife gives a pleasing result without bruising and squashing the product. A tomato cut with a blunt instrument looks like murder.

Senses

When cooking with one's senses, leave taste until last. First listen for when a rolling boil changes to a *plock plock*, as in porridge or a thick soup. Then smell the aroma of something almost done as the flavours have developed, or sniff for any suggestion of burning; the nose is objective about good or bad smells. Between your fingers, feel the graininess disappear from couscous or test the tenderness of a cooked kidney bean. Look to see the colours and consistency change in a dish, for example, when tomatoes in a stew or sauce are well-cooked, the brightness becomes dusky. Lastly, taste: the tongue is a great seducer; gratification and pleasure can deceive one's critical faculties in cooking.

Onion and garlic smells on the hands: as raw onion smells give me a headache, I usually wear gloves for this but if I've forgotten, I wash my hands immediately in cold water first with a spoonful of sugar, then soap. I scrub the chopping board with a spoonful of salt and a lemon skin.

While on the subject of onion, it is interesting to note that many cuisines have specific ways of cutting vegetables. In Lebanese cooking an onion is usually sliced in wings – the bulb is halved and each thin slice must contain a fragment from the core of the onion, sliced outward from the centre.

Grated or Shredded

Where the instruction is for an ingredient to be grated, use a grater. Shredded ingredients should be run through a food processor. Grating ingredients achieves a fine to medium result. Shredding them achieves a coarse result, used in, for example, Eggplant Patties.

Sweating

Most vegetables have a high water content, mushrooms and eggplant, for example, contain well over 70 per cent water. Slow cooking or sweating evaporates some of that water and helps to concentrate the aromas, rounding and enriching the flavours of vegetarian dishes.

Of course, some vegetables, like mushrooms or okra, also do well tossed in a wok on a high heat, but here I want to show how a busy person can make a string of dishes from the same base. I use onion, carrot and celery; if there's turnip, parsnip or leek around, they can be added. I prepare a large quantity and freeze in two-cup portions for a quick start to a winter dinner.

This was always a favourite in the classes, especially with those who feared that vegetarians have to spend hours cooking. In a three-hour class we began by making the sweated vegetable base and then, in very short order, produced, from that base, half a dozen dishes, each with a distinctive flavour. Aside from these we also made three or four other dishes: lunch was a feast of ten different courses!

Sweated Vegetable Mix Base

Eight Cups

6 large carrots, peeled
1 large onion, peeled
6 large sticks celery, leaves removed
2 bay leaves
3 tablespoons olive oil
½ teaspoon salt

Grate all vegetables and tip into a large saucepan with oil, salt and bay leaves. Cover and leave on lowest heat for up to 45 minutes, if necessary, to reduce and soften somewhat.

One Cup

1 large carrot, peeled
1 medium onion, peeled
3 sticks celery, leaves removed
1 bay leaf
2 tablespoons oil
pinch of salt

Grate all vegetables and tip into a saucepan with oil, salt and bay leaf. Cover and leave on lowest heat for up to 20 minutes, if necessary, to reduce and soften somewhat.

Corn and Bean Loaf

Loaf

2 cups Sweated Vegetable Mix Base
1 egg, beaten
⅔ cup bean stock (or water)
1 cup cornflour
2 teaspoons baking powder
2 cups cooked or tinned beans
salt

Topping

1 teaspoon paprika
1 medium tomato, diced
1 tablespoon parmesan
pinch of dried thyme

Spread the sweated vegetable mix into a 20-cm-square, 10-cm-deep oven dish. Mix the egg with the stock, cornflour, baking powder and salt. Add the beans and pour over the vegetables. Sprinkle the loaf with paprika, top with the tomato, parmesan and thyme and bake at 180°C until set. Serve warm with a crisp salad and spicy chilli sauce.

Omelette with Sweated Vegetables

2 cups Sweated Vegetable Mix Base
1 tablespoon oil
2 tablespoons chopped parsley
1 tablespoon chopped mint
pinch of salt
pinch of pepper
6 free-range eggs, lightly beaten
lemon wedges, to serve
chat potatoes, to serve

Heat the oil in a medium saucepan and add the vegetables with the herbs and seasonings. Once heated through, pour the eggs over and stir from time to time over medium heat until set. Serve with wedges of lemon and chat potatoes.

Lima Bean Soup

2 cups Sweated Vegetable Mix Base
1 tin (410 g) lima beans
½ cup chopped parsley
boiling water
cheesy croutons, to serve

Mix all ingredients and boil for about 10 minutes and serve with cheesy croutons.

Vegetable Soup

2 cups Sweated Vegetable Mix Base
1 tablespoon tomato paste
2 cups boiling water
handful of penne pasta
1 tablespoon basil pesto
2 tablespoons parmesan, grated, for garnish

Bring all, except parmesan, to the boil in a medium saucepan, adding extra water if desired. Cook for 10 minutes and serve with parmesan.

Pasta with Red Lentils

2 cups Sweated Vegetable Mix Base
500 g penne pasta
2 cups red lentils, cooked
1 tin (410 g) crushed tomatoes and juice
1 cup ricotta cheese
fresh basil leaves
black pepper, to taste
salt
parmesan, to serve
salad, to serve

While the pasta is boiling, mix the rest of the ingredients. Stir these through the cooked pasta, heat in the microwave for 5 minutes on high (or in a conventional oven at 200°C for 20 minutes) and serve with parmesan and a green salad.

Lasagne with Red Lentils

2 cups Sweated Vegetable Mix Base
2 cups red lentils, cooked
1 cup ricotta cheese
1 small bunch of fresh basil leaves, broken
pinch of dried oregano
pinch of salt
pinch of black pepper
bottle (750 mL) tomato pasta sauce
box (250 g) lasagne sheets
½ cup parmesan, grated, for top

Mix the vegetables, lentils, ricotta, herbs and seasoning. Put a small spoonful of pasta sauce in a baking dish and layer the lasagne sheets with the filling. Pour the pasta sauce over the top, cover with parmesan and bake at 190° C for about 40 minutes. Serve with a green salad or steamed vegetables.

Oat Patties with Celery, Carrot, and Onion

2 cups Sweated Vegetable Mix Base
pinch of salt
ground black pepper
1 tablespoon chopped thyme
1 tablespoon chopped marjoram
1 small onion, finely chopped
1 clove garlic, crushed
½ vegetable stock cube in 2 tablespoons hot water
2 tablespoons olive oil
2 cups quick oats

Knead all the ingredients to make a paste. Form into patties and bake on a baking tray lined with baking paper at 200°C, until crisped. Serve with a spicy tomato sauce.

Freekeh Patties with Rich Mushroom Sauce

Freekeh *is smoked, green wheat, rich in protein, vitamins and minerals. The sauce also goes very well with Kibbe Paté.*

Rich Mushroom Sauce

1 small onion, finely chopped
1 tablespoon olive oil
pinch of sugar
pinch of hot chilli
pinch of pepper
pinch of pimento (allspice)
pinch of cinnamon
3 tablespoons tomato paste
½ cup boiling water
2 cups mushrooms, grilled
2 tablespoons pine nuts, lightly toasted
yoghurt, to serve
salad, to serve

Sauté the onion, add the spices, then the tomato paste thinned with water. Bring to the boil, add the mushrooms and nuts and set aside.

Patties

1 cup Sweated Vegetable Mix Base
2 cups potato, mashed
1 clove garlic, crushed
1 cup raw *freekeh*, boiled to make almost 3 cups cooked
1 teaspoon salt
pinch of pepper

Knead all the ingredients to make a paste. Form this into 6 large patties and bake at 200°C for about 10 minutes, just to crisp the exterior. Serve with Rich Mushroom Sauce, yoghurt and salad leaves.

Artichoke

The globe artichoke is actually the flower bud of a giant thistle, the choke being the immature stamens of the flower. After boiling, peel the strings off the stalk and enjoy the marrow from the core, as well as the globe and its rich bottom. In Lebanese grocers you can buy frozen artichoke bottoms, which are delicious in a lemony stew.

Jerusalem (artichoke) is a corruption of 'girasol', which means sunflower: this is the tuber of a sunflower-like plant that has an artichoke flavour. The Jerusalem artichoke is rich in inulin (natural insulin) and very low GI, but can cause a bit of gas. They are a good source of potassium, calcium, magnesium and protein.

Besan Flour

Besan flour, widely used in Indian cooking, is made of ground chickpeas and is a good source of magnesium and potassium, adding protein as well. It is obtainable from Indian and Middle Eastern grocers.

Chat

Chat in India, is a snack: wedges of fruit or a bowl of chickpeas are dressed with a blend of spices. The main ingredient of chat masala is black salt – a pinkish, unrefined mineral salt with a strong sulphur flavour, mined in India. You can purchase the mixture at an Asian or Indian grocer.

Eggplant

Eggplant (*Solanum melongena*) is a nightshade (like potatoes, tomatoes and capsicum) and has many names: eggfruit, elephant's balls, aubergine, *brinjal, melitzane, buttenjen, melanzane, vambothu, makhua ling, terung* and *berengena*. It is a smooth, waxy skinned fruit ranging in size from a cherry tomato through to a rock melon, with lanky or lady finger shapes in between. Grown and used throughout Asia, the Mediterranean and Middle East, it ranges in colour from dark purple, paler purple to mauve, cream and even white. Pink and white striped fruit look marvellous in the vegetable rack.

Eggplant contains magnesium, potassium and vitamin C. They should always be firm, without depressions, brown patches or holes bored by worms happily munching away at the heart. Although it is a summer crop, in Australia they are available throughout the year, grown in warmer parts of the country during winter.

Eggs

I only ever use certified free-range eggs and make a point of asking for them in cafes and restaurants.

Garlic

Various ingredients that seem remarkably different, these are members of the Liliaceae family: garlic (*Allium sativum*), leek (*Allium porrum*), onion (*Allium cepa*), Chinese garlic chives (*Allium odorum*), and chives (*Allium Schoeneprasum*).

Russian garlic (elephant garlic), so-called because each clove can be the size of a whole head of regular garlic, is a member of the leek family.

In some cultures, the healing properties of this family border on the mystical. Allicin, a powerful bactericide, is present in noticeable quantities, along with sulphur and B and C vitamins.

Garlic also speeds up the digestive process, but some people complain of heartburn from eating garlic. Try removing the small green shoot in the clove, as it can cause indigestion.

My favourite garlic crusher is a small, wooden mortar and pestle bought in a Lebanese grocer. Drop the cloves into the bowl and squash them with the flattened end of the pestle. Sprinkle with a little sea salt and keep pounding until you have a smooth paste.

Above all, garlic must be fresh. Discard browned or bruised cloves. Australian grown garlic is of a very high quality.

Renee's Greek-style Garlic Paste (Skorthalia)

My cousin Renee is married to a Greek man from Lesbos. They run a marvellous bed and breakfast called Mount Joy, in Jeffreys Bay, South Africa's answer to Byron Bay. Her meals are feasts that surfies and gourmands alike celebrate and remember, long after they have moved on.

- 8 cloves garlic, crushed with 1 teaspoon salt
- 5 medium potatoes, boiled
- 1 cup olive oil
- 1 tablespoon lemon juice

Mash the potatoes and put them in a food processor. With the motor still running, gradually add oil in a continuous stream until the mixture is thick and smooth. Add the garlic and lemon juice in the same way, and more salt if desired.

Grains

It is a good idea to include a variety of grains and seeds in the diet. It is good to know of the varieties if you have allergies.

Amaranth

A relative of the cockscomb, leaves and seeds are used; the red flowers are used as a colouring.

Barley

A cereal grain. Pearl barley is lightly polished and used in soups or pilaffs.

Buckwheat

Buckwheat (*kasha* in Eastern Europe) has no relation to wheat; it is a seed used as a cereal and is rich in protein and minerals. Good for coeliacs.

Corn

Corn starch is sometimes called corn flour. Cornmeal, *mieliemeel* or instant polenta can all be used interchangeably. *Samp* is cracked corn; *mielierys* is riced corn – ground *samp* that looks like pearled grains. Most of these are available from South American and South African grocers.

Millet

A grain suitable for coeliacs.

Quinoa

A protein-rich seed, originally from Peru, quinoa is used as a grain. If avoiding wheat, quinoa can be used in *tabbouleh* instead of *burghul.*

Rice

Brown, white, red, long grain, short grain, husked, sticky, par-boiled, flaked, rolled or ground.

I use Arborio or short grain risotto-style rice in some of the stuffed vegetables; otherwise, I prefer fragrant white basmati, which has a medium GI, better than the other refined grains.

Rye

A relative of barley and wheat.

Sorghum

A grass raised for animal and human feed; *maltabella* porridge in South Africa is made from malted sorghum.

Spelt

Sometimes called early wheat, as it seems to be the grain from which our wheat was hybridised.

Teff

A grass, native to Ethiopia; the seed is ground to make injera, a spongy bread for sopping up gravies.

Wheat and By-products

Ordinary corn and wheat flour, wholemeal and sifted plain flour, are used in Lebanese breads. Over time, other derivatives of the basic product have found their way into this ancient cuisine, for example, semolina and *freekeh* (green wheat). A long time ago, in Lebanese villages, when the stores of wheat ran out and the new crop was yet to be harvested, the *freekeh* (or *farik*) was cut and the chaff, set alight. The smoky flavoured remaining grains were separated from the ashes.

Today, the process continues and the result is used in pilaffs, stuffings or salads. More than *burghul* or regular wheat, it has good protein levels as well as calcium, iron, potassium and zinc. Produced in South Australia, it is marketed as *freekeh.*

Semolina ('heart of wheat') is another important wheat product, used in Lebanese cakes, especially *ma'amoul*, which is readily available in Lebanese patisseries.

Burghul

This is how it is made from scratch – my mother and her mother's method.

6 cups wheat berries

In a large saucepan, cover wheat with water and boil until the skins crack and the berries are tender. Drain and spread out on cloths in the sun to dry. This can take up to three days. Grind fine, medium or coarse and store for *kibbe*, *kishk*, *tabbouleh* and other salads.

Washing Burghul

Place the required amount into a bigger bowl and run water in to cover well. Stir and allow to settle. Pour off whatever dust has floated to the surface and drain. Add four times the amount of fresh water (1 cup *burghul* needs 4 cups water) to cover and soak for 30 minutes, then drain and squeeze out excess water and use as required.

KISHK (TRAHANAS)

Kishk *is fermented yoghurt and* burghul. *This recipe is how my mother and her mother made it.*

5 cups *burghul*
enough yoghurt to wet *burghul*
2 or 3 teaspoons salt

Moisten the *burghul* with the yoghurt until it forms a doughy consistency. Cover for 2–3 days, stirring daily until it starts to sour. On the fourth day, add the salt and more yoghurt and stir daily until sour for another 10–12 days. Spread out in lumps on cloths in the sun to dry. Turn and break up lumps every 2–3 hours. After 3 days, grind and store in the refrigerator for later use as a sauce or a savoury porridge.

HERBS

If you are fortunate enough to be able to grow a few herbs, remember to pick them in the morning before the sun has reached them, or a couple of hours after the sun has left them.

Generally, one teaspoon of dried herbs is equal to one tablespoon of fresh herbs. Marjoram and sage are exceptions: they are too strong; a small half teaspoon of these dried is enough. The flavours of basil and mint are quite different flavours when dried. Dried parsley and coriander have very little flavour.

I often use a tablespoon of chopped chives in a salad, instead of onion or garlic.

When using herbs, if you don't have what is suggested, look for equivalent flavours: for marjoram, add a pinch of thyme to dried oregano; for rosemary, use thyme with a pinch of powdered bay.

In Lebanese and Middle Eastern cooking, the most commonly used herbs are coriander, dill, mint, parsley, purslane, tarragon and thyme.

Purslane or pigweed (*ba'lie*), a member of the *Mesembryanthemum* family, is a small succulent whose pink stalks are rich in lycopene. It is an excellent plant source of omega-3. Essential for an authentic *fatousch* salad, purslane is obtainable from Lebanese green grocers.

Basil for Winter

1 large bunch of fresh basil, washed, stalks removed
1 clove garlic
pinch of salt
3 tablespoons olive oil

Put the garlic and salt in a food processor and chop. Add basil leaves and mill with oil. Freeze in an ice tray. 1 cube equals 1 tablespoon for soups, salads, pizzas.

Basil Pesto Pat's Recipe

Pat had an Italian husband and I am certain her cooking beat his sisters' hands down.

1 cup fresh basil leaves
small handful of parsley
3 tablespoons pine nuts, toasted (or walnuts)
pinch of ground pepper
2 tablespoons parmesan cheese
1 clove garlic
about 6 tablespoons olive oil

Mill all ingredients in a processor while slowly adding the oil to form a paste.

Salsa Verde from my Garden

handful of parsley
handful of oregano
handful of basil
small sprig of marjoram
pinch of tarragon (or fennel)
1 clove garlic, crushed
pinch of salt
pinch of pepper
2 tablespoons lemon juice
4 tablespoons oil

Put all the ingredients into a food processor and mill briefly to a chunky consistency.

Mushrooms

Mushrooms are a great food for vegetarians, even containing some vitamin B12. All sorts of fungi are now available, fresh, tinned or dried. I use dried mushrooms either whole, or finely ground to amplify the mushroom flavour of a dish.

Button mushrooms are great for pickling or currying. Large field mushrooms are good for stuffing or slicing and grilling. Portobelloes have a great flavour; in autumn, the rust coloured pine ring mushrooms are lovely just sautéed in a little oil and served with chopped parsley and lemon juice.

Grilled Mushrooms

Delicious as is, or in a sauce or salad.

500 g chopped button mushrooms
½ teaspoon salt
2 tablespoons olive oil

Place mushrooms in a roasting pan, sprinkle salt and oil and place under grill for 7 minutes. Turn over and grill for a further 5 minutes. Turn off and allow to cool completely.

Mushrooms Grilled and Dried

These crispy, chewy and salty bits with a strong mushroom flavour are good with drinks.

400 g portobello mushrooms, sliced very thinly
sprinkling of good salt
3 tablespoons olive oil

Spread slices in large pan, and sprinkle with salt and oil. Put under hot grill for about 8 minutes, until they look cooked. Turn off the grill and leave in the oven for a few hours until cold.

Okra

An attractive plant, growing to about one and a half metres, the okra plant has a pretty yellow flower with a dark centre. Okra is a mallow, related to hibiscus, cotton and cottonwood trees, like the old ones on the beachfront at Byron Bay. It is grown all over Africa and Asia. In the southern United States, okra is used as a thickener in gumbos.

Okra pods should be small, no more than seven centimetres in length – after that they are stringy, with little flesh. It is delicious fried, stewed or curried and lemon juice breaks the slime.

Okra is also related to *Melokhia*, genus *corchorus*, grown for its jute. The melokhia leaves, rich in minerals and vitamins, are made into a soup in Cyprus, Egypt and Lebanon, with garlic, oil and coriander; in Lebanon it is served with vinegared onions – a pot of slime only for accustomed palates.

Olives

According to my mother and both grandmothers, to obtain the correct salinity for olives, put a whole egg into a jug and fill with cool water. Slowly and gently stir in salt until the egg floats: that is the correct saltiness for olives.

Pickled Black Olives Kalamata-style

Kalamata olives
vinegar
water
salt
olive oil

Slit the olives on one side with a sharp blade and leave in salt water for 10–14 days, changing the salt water every 2 days or so. Taste the olives before that time to see if the bitterness has gone. Bring to the boil 1 part vinegar and 2 parts water with salt to taste. Pack the olives into small jars and pour hot solution over. Top with oil and leave to cure, tasting from time to time.

Salt-cured Black Olives

Black, Spanish Queen, Kalamata or large mission – any of these types can be prepared using the following method.

olives
vinegar
water
salt
olive oil

Put the unwashed olives in baskets in the sun for about 3 days until they are soft and ripe, bringing them in at night. Shake up the baskets well every day. When the olives are soft enough, wash, dry and salt them heavily, then cover and keep turning and shaking them up daily, even twice a day for about 10 days until they are really black. They are now getting crinkly. Wash the salt off once, put them in bottles, cover with salt water using the egg test, add a little vinegar and top with oil.

Half-green or Jumbo Spanish Queen Olives

olives
water
salt
lemon juice
olive oil

Bang the olives in a cloth to split. Wash once. Put into plain water for about 4 days, changing water daily. If they are still bitter, leave them for 1–2 days more. When most of the bitterness has gone, pickle in salt water using the egg test. Serve in a bowl with lemon juice, olive oil and a pinch of salt to taste.

Oil

I use only extra virgin olive oil in all my cooking. Sometimes, if I have fresh macadamia or avocado oil from the North Coast, I use them in salad dressings. Macadamia oil can be used in baking, instead of butter.

Pomegranate

In a hurry, for myself, I sometimes dribble a teaspoonful of Pomegranate Molasses Dressing over a dish of salad leaves and toss with a teaspoonful of olive oil. Use as balsamic vinegar – finely chopped tomatoes and avocado dressed simply with Pomegranate Molasses Dressing; sliced strawberries can be drizzled with Pomegranate Molasses Dressing.

Pomegranate Molasses Dressing (Dibs Romaine)

Pure, concentrated juice from pomegranates is great for dressings and readily obtainable from Middle Eastern grocers.

2 tablespoons pomegranate molasses
2 tablespoons white wine vinegar
(or lemon juice)
3 tablespoons olive oil
pinch of salt
pinch of pepper

Mix up well and use as desired.

Shallots

In New South Wales, shallots are pencil-thin onions with green tops, not to be confused with spring onions, which are white, globe onions with green tops.

Spices

In Lebanese cooking, the spices of choice are mostly a blend of pimento (allspice), cinnamon, black or white pepper, cumin and coriander.

Cassia/Cinnamon

When a recipe calls for cinnamon sticks, I use cassia sticks, which are sold in Indian grocers as cinnamon sticks – it is actually the dark coloured bark of the cassia tree, a close relative of cinnamon; it is rather more astringent than cinnamon quills which I find too sweet; if using cinnamon quills, use much less.

When using spices, look for equivalent flavours if you don't have what is suggested, substitute just a little of something else: for example, mace, use a little nutmeg; for cloves, add a pinch of cinnamon to pimento.

Buy whole or ground spices at a Lebanese or Indian grocer, anywhere where there is a high turnover and the product is not extended by the addition of starch.

Pimento (Allspice)

Not to be confused with mixed spice or American pimiento. Used ground or as whole berries.

Sumac

A ruby-coloured coarse powder made from the dried red berry of the sumac tree; a relative of the Rhus, it is native to Iran and Iraq; astringent, it is an excellent souring agent if lemons are in short supply. I love it on rice.

Tahini

Tahini is often called sesame mayonnaise, creamed sesame seeds – in reality it is none of those things: it is plain finely ground sesame seeds; sometimes one finds a product called tahina – this may have added garlic and lemon – read the label.

Unhulled sesame seeds make a darker coloured tahini; Lebanese recipes require the lighter one; tahini is very rich in calcium.

Tahini with loads of added sugar, is the main ingredient of halva.

Tahini Sauce

The basis of humous and babbaganouje, use on any vegetables and very good with stuffed vegetables.

1 cup tahini
100 mL lemon juice
1 clove garlic, crushed
½ teaspoon salt
100 mL water

In a food processor, blend the tahini, juice, garlic and salt together while slowly adding water to form a velvety sauce.

Vine Leaves

I prefer fresh leaves, the fourth, fifth and sixth on a tendril, before they've been hardened by the wind and sun; blanch in boiling water before use; if using packaged leaves, they should be soaked in cold water and rinsed well to reduce the saltiness.

Yoghurt (Laban and Labne)

Yoghurt is *laban*, and *labne* is drained yoghurt or Lebanese-style smooth cottage cheese. Here is a recipe if you want to make your own *laban*. To make your own *labne*, put your homemade yoghurt into a muslin-lined strainer over a bowl in the fridge for 12–24 hours, or do the same with bought Greek-style yoghurt. Good *labne* can also be bought in Lebanese grocers.

1 L full cream milk
3 tablespoons Greek-style yoghurt

Heat milk to boiling and allow to cool to the point where one cannot leave a finger in for too long; stir some of the warm milk into the yoghurt and then pour all back into the saucepan and stir thoroughly. Cover and wrap well or enclose in a wondercushion to keep warm for at least eight hours. Once it has set, refrigerate and use as desired.

ZA'ATER

A blend of Lebanese thyme, sesame seeds, sumac and salt; make into a paste with olive oil, spread on bread dough and bake like a pizza; or use as a dip for toasts with drinks.

Excellent *za'ater* is available in Lebanese grocery stores: the greener in colour, the better.

ZUCCHINI

Black (actually dark green) and gray; the black ones are not really suitable for stuffing as they break; the gray ones stay whole when stuffed and cooked. A zucchini corer can be obtained from a Lebanese grocer; tennis ball shaped zucchinis are easy to hollow with a melon baller. Choko is useful to extend zucchini in a frittata or simple stew – it takes on the surrounding flavours very well.

Good cooking is an alchemical process in which a spirited cook uses techniques to achieve an aromatic result.

You cannot consume beyond your appetite.
The other half of the loaf belongs to the other
person and there should remain a little
bread for the chance guest.

– Kahlil Gibran

Digesting my Life

I can't be certain what solid food first passed my infant lips. But most likely it was the sour and salty *m'finu* pressed into my gummy babble by the loving fingers of Rosie, my Xhosa nursemaid. '*Sela, mama, sela,*' she exhorted me to swallow the green and white paste of African spinach, cornmeal and sour milk: 'Drink, mother, drink,' she said, in the style of Arab and African cultures that call girl children, mother and boys, dadda or daddy.

Myself, aged seven months.

She would have untied me from her back and swung me around to sit in the folds of her capacious lap, her huge breasts, fleshy pillows that propped my flopping infancy. From that porridge I grew into the more solid *ngqush* or *samp* (cracked corn), and could join Rosie's daughter, Gladys, under the loquat tree where the sticky golden fruit occupied our afternoons. We swallowed the flesh in a quest for the brown marble seeds that we spat at each other.

When I was five, Rosie and all her family went away. Not only did she take her children, but she took my language as well: I became silent and refused to speak. I seemed to have decided that if I couldn't speak Xhosa, I would not speak English with my inside family, Afrikaans with the other maids, or Arabic with Granny. But Granny was not going to be defeated by me: '*Do'ee, do'ee,*' she coaxed as I craned my pursed lips out of her reach until her nicotined fingers won and plugged the inside of my cheek with a paste of bread and fried eggplant: 'Taste it, taste it.' She reached me in a most Lebanese way with food and language, teaching me to cook alongside her as she described all her actions in Arabic.

In that same year, housemaid Sarah fed me curries and cigarettes, so that by the time I was six I had become used to unexpected explosions in my mouth. The insult of spices and chilli grew, by the time I was fifteen, into a passionate love affair.

While I was learning to eat with so many tastes and flavours, I was also learning about hunger and starvation: most of us experienced 'Eat up, eat up!

There are starving children in India and China.' And I thought that must have been true: there were pictures at school of starving children thousands of miles away; why else did Mr Patel and Mr Sent leave India and China to open shops in our street in East London, South Africa?

I began to notice starving children much closer to home. We took family holidays into the country to visit relatives, and when we stopped to buy clay animals from the children beside the road, my parents gasped, 'Look how thin they are, such skinny legs – you children don't know how lucky you are.'

In the early mornings my father taught me to read the newspaper and there I saw photographs of Africans – Xhosa people like my Rosie and her family – in dreadful circumstances. In the courtyard of my home, countless people waited to see my lawyer father – men and old women, many carrying spindly infants whose mothers were in domestic service. They spoke Xhosa to me, relating stories of terrible suffering because of the growing apartheid laws. To Cook's great consternation, I made tea and jam sandwiches for them.

'This child is driving me mad here, always feeding these people, and they come because they know there's food here.' And I stamped my eight-year-old foot and raised my voice. 'But they are hungry, they've walked a long way and now they are waiting for my father.'

As a teenager, I became the family baker and visited my aunts' homes to cook and bake for their freezers. When I first left home, in all of my cooking I drew on my grandmother's earlier constant presence and tutoring in Middle Eastern flavours and techniques: lentils and eggplant intrigued my friends at Rhodes University in Grahamstown. It was also at university that I first encountered malnutrition among the ricket-struck children in the local African township.

Michele, Bertha, myself and Anita. I had already begun learning to cook with Granny.

By the time I was married and running a household in Cape Town, I was convinced of our responsibility as affluent citizens to assist the poor and underprivileged who surrounded us. I began to work in local community organisations encouraging the better heeled to help in the distribution of non-perishable foodstuffs to the squatter camps down the road. The cost of a piece of prime animal for one meal at my table could feed a small family in a poor country for a month. I didn't feel entitled to that, and I became a vegetarian.

Later, as I was raising my allergic children on a vegan diet, I grew more interested in lifestyle as a cause of illness or creator of wellness. My mother had been a natural-health advocate: brown bread, no sugars or fats. We had a little meat, but a traditional Lebanese diet in those days contained plenty of seeds and nuts, grains and legumes and no pork.

Festivals and celebrations around the globe are usually characterised by the food or special drink served, and it is this coming-together that most cultures have in common. In my own past, it was at the huge lunches where thirty or forty of us gathered over baths of *tabbouleh*, *humous* and *babbaganouje* that I experienced the comfort and pleasure of my Lebanese heritage. It was also there at the table that my mother, exhorting restraint, frequently remonstrated: 'You are digging your grave with your teeth.' And it was her wowser attitude that regularly sent my chocoholic father on an after-lunch quest for a 'Cadbury's'. The spices and flavours I use in these recipes, although health-conscious, reveal a *joie de vivre* that inspired the many students who stood with me at my work bench.

Drawn from the poignancy, longing, comfort and delight that I find in my heart's memory, I offer you this small selection of favourite recipes from my own African–Lebanese experience, as taught and prepared in Cecile's Vegetarian Kitchen.

A family braaivleis (barbecue) with baths of tabbouleh, babbaganouje and humous b'tahini, 1957.

The Mezze Table

Cooking with my mother, some of my earliest memories are of the great pleasure and excitement in preparing a *mezze* table for guests.

Mezze is a myriad small bowls, each one adding colour, texture, spice and flavour to make up a universe of food that will tempt even the most resistant appetite. A table of *mezze* and *arak*, an anise-flavoured liqueur, can last from lunchtime to late at night – depending on the flow of sustenance and the fervour of the conversation, which are both usually plentiful in Lebanese gatherings. Breaks from eating can be punctuated by puffs on the *narghile* (bubble pipe). Hot water bubbles steam through the *tombac* (apple-scented tobacco).

Hospitality is the life-blood of this culture where people live in extended-family groups. In such peasant societies, living close to the land where shortages were often keenly felt, whatever one had belonged to everyone and any passersby. From ancient days of long travel in desert places, where welcoming strangers was a sacred and sometimes life-saving act, hospitality has been embedded in the culture. My mother taught us, as she herself had to learn, who to seat where at the table. A man, in our case, our father, always sat at the head. The most important woman, our mother, sat on his right, and the next most important woman, our eldest sister, sat on his left. Men and women were always alternated in the seating arrangements.

Granny Isabel loved her nhargile, especially on a Sunday picnic near the sea.

As I understood it, these were English rules that my mother had gleaned from etiquette books. Some traditionalists didn't invite singles to their table, as that would have upset the balance.

Here in Australia, I seat my guests as I think they'd be comfortable: 'John, please sit here, Bev over there …' I notice a shy guest, behind curling fingers and hunched shoulders, wondering where to sit, and then someone bursts out, 'You South Africans tell us what to do – can't we sit where we like?'

'Of course,' I reply. 'But I only do it so that everyone feels they have a special place and are welcome at the table.'

Wherever you are in the world, a Lebanese will share food with you. An Englishman recently told me, with pleasure, of his first taste of pistachio nuts. He was travelling on a train outside London when a 'foreign' man passed him a handful and showed him how to shell them.

Wherever we are from or wherever we are going, we all appreciate feeling included, whether it be as a stranger on the road or at someone's table.

Come, let us assemble a feast. From your nearest Lebanese grocer, buy a selection of black and green olives: bowls of gleaming Kalamatas, shrivelled date olives, Moroccan gems, giant ripe Greek and broken green olives in a bath of lemon and garlic. A selection sits wonderfully well next to a dish of creamy white *labne* (cottage cheese) topped with green olive oil.

Fill the bread basket with folded *markouk* (mountain paper bread) – circles of flat bread and fingers of Turkish, a jug of water and a bottle of *arak*.

Sahtein! For your very good health, I wish you all the pleasures and delights of a Lebanese table.

A mezze feast for the Bangalow Writers' Group.
Photograph by Lisa Sharpe.

Nuts

We are fortunate in Australia to have a great variety of fresh seeds and nuts: Tasmanian walnuts are especially sweet, South Australian almonds are fleshy and crunchy, pecans from the New South Wales north coast are addictive. At Lebanese celebrations, serve walnuts for longevity and almonds for fertility, and this is not a surprise as nuts, high in omega-3 oils, are a great health food.

SOAKED ALMONDS

Follow exactly the same method for walnuts.

1 cup almonds, skin on

Wash the nuts and put them into a glass bowl, cover well with water and refrigerate. They are ready to eat after 24 hours. Serve on a *mezze* table or with breakfast. Change the water daily for use within 3 days.

SALTED ALMONDS (LOHZ)

Nuts are an intrinsic part of the Lebanese diet – salted, plain, roasted and sweet, they feature from the beginning to the end of a meal or a day.

1 cup almonds, skin on
½ teaspoon sea salt
1 tablespoon water

Mix salt and water and moisten all nuts. Place in a microwave bowl and zap on high for 1 minute. Stir and cook for another minute, then stir and test one on the top to see if they are cooked. Leave to cool.

Pepitas (Bizr)

2 cups pumpkin seeds (pepitas), peeled
salt (optional)

Put the seeds into a dry pan and stir over moderate heat until swollen and changing colour. They will crackle and pop in the pan. Leave to cool. Sprinkle with salt if desired.

Using unpeeled seeds, make sure they are thick – thin ones can be empty – and then dry them in hot sun for a few days. Rub off the golden membrane and put into a pan over low to medium heat. Moisten with 1 tablespoon of water and 2 teaspoons of salt and stir slowly for up to half an hour until seeds change colour slightly.

Pickles

A few pickles in the pantry can be served anytime, for lunch, drinks or dinner. Indeed, a plate of colourful pickles is a good digestive aid for the heavier food to follow. The process is simple. Pack vegetables of your choice into a clean glass jar, fill with pickling solution, seal and store until ready to use.

Pickling Solution

250 mL cider vinegar
100 mL olive oil
1 teaspoon salt
12 pimento (allspice) berries
6 whole cloves
100 mL boiling water

Mix all together.

Cabbage

1 white cabbage
pickling solution

Cut a white cabbage in quarters and pickle in the solution. Beetroot may be added for colour. Ready after 1 week.

Capsicum

1 green capsicum
pickling solution

Make a few small holes in the capsicum and bottle whole.

Cucumber

cucumbers
pickling solution

Use the solution for pieces or whole gherkins. Ready after 2 weeks, depending on the size.

Turnip Pickles (Kabees el Lifft)

3 small turnips
1 tiny beetroot
½ cup cider vinegar
½ cup water
1 bay leaf
1 teaspoon coriander seeds
6 pimento (allspice) berries
small chilli
pinch of salt

Score turnip deeply in slices, but not completely through. Put into a glass jar with beetroot. Mix all spices and liquids and pour into the jar and allow to stand for 3 days. Refrigerate after that to retain crispness.

Pickled Lemons after Tess Mallos

Delicious with Spinach Rolls, gallete and pie.

2 large lemons, sliced in ½-cm-thick circles, top to bottom
2 tablespoons salt
1 teaspoon black peppercorns
4 dried bay leaves
2 teaspoons sweet paprika
enough olive oil to fill the jar

Spread lemons on a plate and salt on both sides. Place, sloping, on the drainboard and leave for 24 hours. Put slices into a clean jar layered with paprika, bay leaves and peppercorns. Top up with olive oil, removing air bubbles low down in the jar with a chopstick. Leave in the pantry for 3 weeks.

Eggplant Patties

Granny made these with the innards from eggplants she'd hollowed out for stuffing. She deep-fried them, but my health-conscious mother turned her nose up at that. So I tried and succeeded in baking them instead. Zucchini can be used in place of eggplant.

2 medium eggplants, peeled and shredded
1 medium onion, shredded
2 tomatoes, shredded
2 tablespoons chopped mint
4 tablespoons chopped parsley
salt
pepper
½ teaspoon cinnamon
1 teaspoon pimento (allspice)
2 tablespoons olive oil
1 cup flour
1 teaspoon baking powder
1 egg

Add the rest of the ingredients to the shredded eggplant, onion and tomato and mix well. Bake spoonfuls in an oiled pan or use baking paper. They will cook in 20–25 minutes at 190°C. Serve at room temperature with avocado, chilli and yoghurt.

Broad Bean Patties (Falafel)

1 kg peeled, dried baby broad beans (sometimes called tik peas)
3 cloves garlic
1 large onion
small handful of parsley
small bunch of coriander
2 tablespoons olive oil
2 teaspoons ground cumin
1 teaspoon bi-carb
½ teaspoon hot chilli
1 teaspoon salt
3 tablespoons olive oil (if baking)
pinch of pepper

Soak the beans for 24 hours, changing the water twice. Put the drained beans in the bowl of the food processor in two lots and mill until a fine paste results. Add the rest of the ingredients except olive oil halfway through. Blend thoroughly and tip out into a mixing bowl. Knead by hand, form into patties or small balls and bake on greased baking paper at 200°C for about 15 minutes, or deep-fry until brown.

Dips and Spreads

Coloured cloaks for breads and crudités, dips are a good way of presenting extra vegetables that children will enjoy. Medical research suggests that the more colours on the plate, the longer the life.

Beetroot Dip

4 medium beetroots, boiled, peeled and finely grated
1 medium red onion, peeled and grated
½ cup plain Greek-style yoghurt
1 cup tzatziki

Mix all together well. Chill and serve as a dip or side salad.

Black Olive Tapenade

I prefer a chunky paste and usually use plain Greek black or pitted Kalamata olives.

400 g pitted black olives
1 tablespoon olive oil
1 tablespoon red wine vinegar

Put olives into the bowl of a food processor and pulse briefly to retain chunkiness. Add oil and vinegar.

Chilli Refresher

Lemon and tomato neutralise capsicain, the burn element in chilli.

1 cup seeded bell chilli (or red Dutch chillies)
100 mL lemon juice
1 medium tomato, seeded
1 teaspoon salt

Blend all ingredients in a food processor until soupy. Serve with *humous* or Broad Bean Dip.

Broad Bean Dip

2 cups soaked, rinsed, peeled and dried broad beans
2 teaspoons ground cumin
1 clove garlic, crushed
salt
pepper
2 tablespoons olive oil
1 tablespoon white wine vinegar

Boil the beans until tender, then add cumin, garlic, salt and pepper, oil and vinegar. Blend. Serve with chilli and yoghurt.

Chickpeas with Tahini (Humous b'tahini)

4 cups chickpeas, well-cooked
200 mL tahini
175 mL lemon juice
2 teaspoons salt
olive oil
paprika

Liquidise all ingredients to form a smooth paste. Spread on a platter, garnish with oil and paprika.

Eggplant Dip (Babbaganouje)

A real smoky flavour. Should be a chunky consistency, or use food processor for a smooth paste.

3 medium eggplants
175 mL lemon juice
1 teaspoon salt
200 mL tahini
1 clove garlic, crushed
sweet onion, to serve
bread, to serve

Grill eggplants over a flame until thoroughly blackened (7–10 minutes). Place in a microwave dish and cook in the microwave on high for 7 minutes. Slit and scoop out the soft pulp. Pour over lemon juice and salt, and beat with tahini. Chill and serve with wedges of sweet onion and bread.

Harissa Paste

A spark for the palate.

1 cup medium to hot chillies, chopped
1 red capsicum, roasted, skinned and deveined
8 cloves garlic
1 teaspoon caraway seeds
2 teaspoons ground coriander
1 teaspoon ground cumin
½ cup fresh mint leaves
1 tablespoon balsamic vinegar
pinch of salt
little oil

Put all ingredients into the bowl of a food processor and mill until a saucy consistency.

Walnut Spread

I only use fresh Tasmanian walnuts that I shell myself. The difference is amazing, as they are so sweet.

2 slices wholemeal bread
½ cup vegetable stock (made with ½ a cube)
2 cups walnuts
1 clove garlic, crushed
pinch of white pepper
1 level teaspoon paprika
1 tablespoon olive oil
1 tablespoon pomegranate molasses

Moisten bread with stock and put into a food processor with the rest of the ingredients and process until quite smooth.

Carrot Dip with Dill Seed

Not really Lebanese, but so bright next to the beetroot.

2 cups carrot, boiled and mashed
1 small teaspoon dill seeds
1 clove garlic, crushed
½ cup *labne* (or sour cottage cheese)
2 tablespoons sour cream
2 teaspoons wine vinegar
pinch of salt
ground pepper

Blend all ingredients well, chill and serve with spicy crackers.

Sprout Spread

The enthusiasm with which sprouts send out a tap root, beginning new life in a jar in a dark cupboard, reminds me of some of my friends – like Irene, unbridled liveliness, no matter what!

1 clove garlic
½ teaspoon salt
4 cups mung beans (or lentil sprouts)
3 tablespoons tahini
juice of 1 lemon

Process the garlic and salt, add sprouts, tahini and lemon. Process into a chunky paste.

Auntie's Pine Nut Sauce with Garlic

(Taratoor b'snobar)

My mother had banned garlic in our home; she feared that anyone smelling it on her would label her as a foreigner. Because of this, Auntie Moine came to the rescue and gave me her recipe for taratour b'snobar *(Lebanese pine nut sauce with garlic).*

1 cup toasted pine nuts

4 cloves garlic, pounded with a pinch of sea salt

125 mL water

2 thick slices stale white bread, soaked in water and squeezed

4 tablespoons lemon juice

Blend nuts and garlic with a little of the water until you get a smooth paste. Continue to run the motor while adding the bread and lemon juice. Allow to stand a while before using.

Salads

Lebanese cuisine is peppered with salads of both raw and cooked ingredients – garden salads, *tabbouleh*, *fatousch*. No matter how laden a table, there is always a well-dressed raw salad.

Farmer's Salad with Croutons (Fatousch)

4 ripe tomatoes, chopped
8 shallots, chopped including tops
3 gherkin cucumbers (not pickled), peeled and diced
6 red radishes, sliced
4 leaves cos lettuce, shredded
½ cup chopped mint
½ cup chopped parsley
1 cup purslane (ba'lie) leaves
salt
pepper
sprinkling of sumac
sprinkling of pimento (allspice)

Dressing

25 mL lemon juice
75 mL pomegranate molasses
50 mL olive oil
3 cups fried or toasted croutons of thin Lebanese bread

Mix salad ingredients together, sprinkle with spices and toss with dressing. Serve with croutons on top.

Purslane Salad (Ba'lie)

bunch of purslane, washed and roughly broken
pinch of salt
pinch of pepper
2 tablespoons pomegranate molasses

Put leaves into a bowl, sprinkle with salt and pepper and drizzle with molasses.

Fried Lettuce Salad (Hindbeh)

Traditionally made with endive or other bitter leaves.

oil
2 large onions, sliced
10 large outer leaves of lettuce, shredded
bunch of coriander, chopped
juice of 1 lemon
salt
pepper

Put a little oil into a saucepan and fry the onions. Add the shredded lettuce and mix well. Add chopped coriander and simmer on low for about 45 minutes until tender. Finish off with seasoning and lemon juice and serve cold.

Burghul Salad (Tabbouleh) with Vine Leaves

125 g soaked and squeezed *burghul*, washed and soaked for 20 minutes, then squeezed dry
12 young grape vine leaves tightly rolled into a cigar and shredded finely
small bunch of mint, chopped
large bunch of flat-leaf parsley, finely chopped
½ bunch of shallots, chopped
4 red tomatoes, finely diced
80 mL lemon juice
25 mL olive oil
salt
pepper
pinch of pimento (allspice)

Mix all together and serve with small vine leaves in order to scoop up a mouthful.

Shangleesh Salad

Shangleesh is a cheese made of dried yoghurt, flavoured with a stronger cheese, chilli and oregano.

1 ball shangleesh
2 medium tomatoes, finely chopped
1 medium Spanish onion, finely chopped
pepper
olive oil

Break cheese up and mix with salad ingredients, dress with pepper and olive oil and serve.

Watercress Salad (Jarjer)

In my broken Arabic, I once ordered a salad of sarsoor *(cockroach) – I'll never confuse these two words again!*

Salad

bunch of watercress, picked over, washed and de-stalked
4 medium red tomatoes, diced
2 Lebanese cucumbers, sliced
bunch (6 or 8) of small red radishes, sliced (or 1 cup thinly sliced *daikon* – long white radish)
4 shallots, sliced including tops

Dressing

1 tablespoon of pomegranate molasses (or 1 tablespoon white wine vinegar with a pinch of sugar)
1 tablespoon lemon juice
pinch of salt
pinch of white pepper
2 tablespoons olive oil

Toss all ingredients, shake dressing together, dress and serve.

Vine leaves stuffed with rice and herbs (dolmades in Greece), are a sign that one is eating the food of the eastern Mediterranean. Tender leaves should be harvested before sun and wind have done their damage. In South Africa, my mother once fooled a guest at the table and told him they were caterpillars, the big fat green ones that hide in the grape vine.

Vine Leaves with Herbed Rice (Warra Einab)

If using brined leaves, soak in cold water for a few hours to reduce saltiness.

250 g vine leaves, blanched

Filling

1 cup basmati rice, washed
2 tablespoons fresh dill, chopped
2 tablespoons chopped mint
2 tablespoons chopped parsley
3 tablespoons pine nuts
1 large onion, finely chopped
1 teaspoon salt
1 teaspoon sumac
4 tablespoons lemon juice
3 tablespoons olive oil

Mix all ingredients for filling. Spread leaves, underside up, and place a small amount of filling in the centre, at the stalk end. Begin rolling, folding the edges closed. Place a few leaves in the bottom of the saucepan and pack the rolled leaves closely together. Cover with a few more leaves and a little oil. Add enough water to cover and put a plate on top. Bring to the boil and simmer for 45 minutes until the liquid is mostly absorbed. Allow to stand and cool. Unpack into a serving bowl, adding more lemon and oil if desired.

Vine Leaves with Tomato

This is the quick version.

250 g vine leaves – fresh if possible

Filling

1 cup basmati rice, washed
1 large onion, finely chopped
2 tablespoons pine nuts
2 tablespoons tomato paste
2 tablespoons olive oil
2 tablespoons lemon juice
1 teaspoon salt

Mix filling ingredients. Roll leaves and cook as for Vine Leaves with Herbed Rice.

Silverbeet Stalks in Tahini Sauce

bunch of silverbeet stalks, washed, cut into 2.5 cm pieces, steamed till tender
1 cup tahini
100 mL lemon juice
1 clove garlic, crushed
½ teaspoon salt
100 mL water

Blend tahini, juice, garlic and salt while slowly adding water to form a velvety consistency. Dress hot stalks. Allow to cool and serve at room temperature.

Spinach Rolls

Thick and substantial – always served at room temperature.

12 washed and de-stalked silverbeet leaves, blanched to wilt in boiling water (keep stalks)
1 tomato, sliced

Filling

3 tablespoons chickpeas, soaked overnight
4 medium-size ripe tomatoes, finely chopped
1 large onion, finely chopped
⅓ cup chopped mint
⅔ cup chopped parsley
1 cup Arborio rice, washed
1 teaspoon salt
1 teaspoon pimento (allspice)
1 teaspoon sumac
pinch of white pepper
60 mL lemon juice
2 tablespoons olive oil

Cut the spinach leaves in half and lay underside up on a board. Mix the filling ingredients and put 1 tablespoonful onto each leaf. Roll up, leaving ends open. Line a saucepan with the spinach stalks and tomato and arrange rolls close to one another. Cover with boiling water and 1 tablespoon of oil. Place a saucer over the top and simmer gently for 1 hour until the rice is cooked and the liquid is absorbed. Leave to cool in the pot and tip out onto a serving platter. Serve with extra lemon juice and salt if desired.

Spinach Galette

Use the same ingredients as Spinach Rolls.

Lightly oil a 1.5-litre pudding basin. Cover the base and sides with silverbeet leaves and layer with one third of the filling. Create a layer with a few leaves, add more filling and end with leaves. Pour over 2 tablespoons of oil, cover with a plate and set into a saucepan of boiling water. Simmer for about an hour, ensuring the pot doesn't boil dry. Leave to cool completely. Invert the basin onto a serving platter and chill. Serve in wedges.

Oil Pastry

Granny's pastry mimics a yeasted dough – useful for pizzas and pasties.

2 cups self-raising flour
1 teaspoon salt
2 tablespoons oil
warm water

Put flour and salt into the bowl of a food processor. Add oil and spin briefly. Add enough water to form a sticky dough and process for about 4 minutes. Scrape out of the bowl onto a floured board and form into a smooth ball. Cover and allow to rest for a few minutes.

Spinach Pie (using Oil Pastry)

A lovely light meal with yoghurt.

500 g spinach, finely chopped
1 large onion, finely chopped
1 cup mint, chopped
1 cup parsley, chopped
4 medium tomatoes, finely chopped
salt
pepper
cinnamon
sumac
1 teaspoon pimento (allspice)
60 mL lemon juice
2 tablespoons olive oil
1 quantity Oil Pastry

Mix all the ingredients except pastry. Roll the dough and cover the bottom of a large roasting pan. Working fast, to avoid the filling becoming watery and wetting the dough, put filling in, cover with a top layer of dough, stretch to seal the edges, prick, paint with oil and bake at 220°C for about 30 minutes. Remove from the oven and cover with a damp tea towel and allow to cool. Cut and serve cold.

To make cottage cheese (*labne*) from yoghurt (*laban*), put a quantity of yoghurt into a muslin-lined strainer and refrigerate until well-drained – at least twelve hours.

Bought Greek-style yoghurt is excellent in flavour and consistency and, to be honest, saves me a lot of time.

Labne with Chives

On rye toast with olives for breakfast!

1 cup *labne*
2 tablespoons chopped chives

Stir together and use as a spread.

Labne Pie

Individual pies can be made using a bread dough or Oil Pastry. I prefer to use filo and make one large pie that I leave to cool and serve at room temperature, cut into squares. This recipe is for a 15 x 25 cm pan.

12 sheets filo pastry

Filling

250 mL *labne*
1 medium onion, finely chopped
pinch of salt
1 tablespoon olive oil

Mix all ingredients well. Lay 6 sheets of filo in a pan and spread with filling. Cover with 6 more layers and brush lightly with olive oil. Bake at 190°C for about 30 minutes, until browned.

Labne Pizza

1 pre-baked Italian pizza base or an Oil Pastry base
400 g labne
1 medium red onion, sliced in rings
½ cup black olives, pitted
oregano
pepper
sumac
little extra virgin olive oil

Beat *labne* and spread over base. Cover with onion rings, then olives. Sprinkle with seasonings and drizzle with oil. Bake at 200°C for about 30 minutes, until browned.

Labne and Mushroom Pizza

1 pre-baked Italian pizza base or an Oil Pastry base
400 g *labne*
1 cup cooked mushrooms, chopped
2 tablespoons onions, diced and fried
pinch of cinnamon
½ teaspoon pimento (allspice)
salt
pepper
pinch of sumac
1 tablespoon toasted pine nuts

Blend all ingredients and spread over the base. Bake at 200°C for about 30 minutes, until browned.

Labne-stuffed Mushrooms

For cocktails – wheat-free snacks to have with a drink.

24 field mushrooms, about 5 cm in diameter, stalks removed

Filling

250 g *labne*
mushroom stalks, chopped
1 tablespoon onions, diced and fried
pinch of cinnamon
½ teaspoon pimento (allspice)
salt
pepper
pinch of sumac
1 tablespoon toasted pine nuts
olive oil

Mix all filling ingredients, pack into mushrooms, sprinkle with olive oil and bake at 220°C for about 18 minutes, until just browning.

Za'ater means 'thyme' in Arabic. In Australia, what we know as *za'ater* is a ready-made mix of Lebanese thyme, sesame seeds, salt and sumac. *Za'ater* is sprinkled on breads, cottage cheese, crudités and even eaten with boiled eggs for breakfast. Many of the Lebanese pizzerias specialise in warm breads topped with *za'ater* or haloumi cheese.

ZA'ATER

2 tablespoons dried oregano (or Lebanese thyme)
1 tablespoon sesame seeds, toasted
1 level teaspoon sumac
pinch of salt
3 tablespoons olive oil

Combine well and make a paste with olive oil.

ZA'ATER BREADS (M'NAISH)

½ cup *za'ater* powder
4 tablespoons olive oil
1 teaspoon crushed garlic

Mix all ingredients well to form a paste that drips off the spoon. Spread on a pre-baked pizza base OR on thin Lebanese bread or on bread dough and bake at 200°C for about 12–15 minutes, until crisped.

ZA'ATER CRISPS

2 level tablespoons *za'ater* powder
3 tablespoons olive oil
2 large rounds Lebanese bread cut into triangles

Mix za'atar and olive oil to make a paste and spread onto bread. Toast on a baking tray for 10–12 minutes at 200° C.

The ultimate goal of farming is not the growing of crops, but the cultivation and perfection of human beings.

– Masanobu Fukuoka, Natural Farmer

Compost Forever

Auntie Susie taught us to say 'All for the birds and none for the devil' when we scattered breadcrumbs onto the lawn. Whether rats and cockroaches took any notice of our incantation is uncertain, but it eased our well-inculcated guilt about throwing food away. All for the birds and none for the devil – I have not said that for many years, because all food scraps go onto my compost heap.

My octogenarian friend, Carol, regularly wins the garden competitions in Bangalow. Her able assistant, Colin, quotes Satish Kumar, with words to the effect that if you can't make compost, you don't know how to live. Colin and Carol certainly know how to live; as almost self-sufficient gardeners and vegetarians, their evident good health and stamina over long years, speaks volumes.

Compost fits with the Buddhist notion that in life we compost our experiences and feelings – we can grow roses and herbs, or be overtaken by noxious weeds ...

In my tiny garden there are two compost bins into which I discard kitchen waste, some paper products, grass and other soft garden clippings, including my hair, which is safe because it's not dyed. All are layered with a bit of lime and some soil. To accelerate the process, I add seaweed, worm juice or comfrey leaves. After about eight months, I lift the bin and leave the heap exposed for the compost to finally break down and dry out. The empty bin is relocated in the garden where the rich juice from the decomposition process of the new batch will feed surrounding plants. Once the compost is friable, I dig it lightly into the top ten centimetres of my vegetable garden. After a week's rest, I plant seedlings of vegetables I prefer to grow myself – lettuces, spinach and other leaves.

The compost bin is also a great place to recycle those personal journals that were meant for your eyes only! And there is another secret thing I once did in my compost heap that is, sadly, no longer possible in town. When my daughter was born at home, her father was designated to carry the placenta out to the compost heap. Six months later, I fed the lemon tree with that placental compost and on my daughter's first birthday, I handed a basket of the juiciest golden lemons to the doctor who had delivered her in my bedroom.

These and other vegetables, fruits and delights, which have restored the cells of my body daily and given me the energy to continue, came out of the earth. Unlike a dog depositing steamy piles on the nature strip, ours goes down the pipes and is, in some cases, returned to the sea by the sewerage system, limiting public contagion and the spread of pathogens.

But what of the greatest recycling opportunity of all? What to do with this conversion machine, my body, when its functions are stilled? It cannot be flushed down the loo. I don't want it to be buried so deeply that it becomes an anaerobic mess in the earth. Cremation would be my ultimate carbon faux pas. Having eaten fresh food most of my life and avoided chemicals and preservatives, I dream of being useful in death. So I am thinking of natural burial, where my body can assist in the regeneration of a patch of exhausted earth.

Wrapped in a cotton winding sheet, I'd like to be buried in a one-metre-deep hole beneath a tree to provide shade, nests and shelter, to store carbon and eventually grow something nutritious in the organically enriched earth.

My first eggplant, grown bio-dynamically in white, almost sea-sand.

Artichokes, Eggplants, Okra, Tomatoes and Zucchini

As a child, I spent most of my days outside in the garden. We had an extensive vegetable garden with a huge, underground water tank to collect run-off from the roof. The orchard of fruit, pecan and olive trees lead to a poultry yard that was divided into sections for hens, bantams and the Christmas turkey. I spent hours in there sitting on a huge rock, talking to the white leghorns, puffing away on my cigarettes.

My mother's sister, Phyllis, sits on the edge of the burrkie – a pond in the garden for cooling watermelons, grapes and other fruit in blazing Karoo summers.

Jackson or Victor, the gardeners, followed my mother around as she gave instructions for what should be planted, harvested or ploughed up. I trailed along with Askim, the slobbery boxer. Among the vegetables, okra and eggplants were the prettiest. Purslane (or ba'li), commonly called pig-weed, a succulent with pink stems, grew wild between the beds.

My mother's brothers and sister were excellent gardeners – sometimes Granny and I walked around the block to Albert or Mickey's garden. Phyllis was in Queenstown in the karroo where the hot dry summers produced wonderful peaches and marrows, loads of which she'd bring to us at the coast. Granny minced the marrows and made spicy patties. Henry's garden was in the Orange Free State and when he and his family came to the coast for holidays, their gardener would harvest zucchini or melons and send them in crates on the overnight passenger train to us in East London.

Okra was grown every year in our garden; the seeds were planted in September and the harvest began in March. An attractive plant, growing to about 1.5 metres, it has a pretty yellow flower with a dark centre.

Later in life, the climate and soil in Bangalow conspired to give me a fruitful vegetable patch; the year I grew a hedge of Jerusalem artichokes all along the paling fence, I harvested bucketsful that were roasted, steamed, baked and prepared in ways that gave rise to some of these recipes.

Last but not least, eggplant. A member of the *Solanaceae* (or nightshade) family along with potatoes, capsicums and tomatoes, like all nightshades, eggplant can be the food of dreams. It is a soulful vegetable, with which passionate cooks can play most creatively using all of their skills, herbs and spices, as well as techniques other than frying, to produce delicious results.

To salt or not to salt – I no longer salt.

Antonio Carluccio explains, in *Antonio Carluccio's Vegetables*, that 'as the bitterness has been bred out … Better to spend more time eating aubergines than preparing them.'

When properly cooked, the fork should pierce the skin as it would a pat of butter. If undercooked and a sharp knife is necessary to cut into it, it becomes the stuff of nightmares – a pet-hate launching me into a tirade about cooks who should know better. I think the alkaloids in under-cooked eggplant are toxic and provoke ill humour in the diner!

The microwave is useful in some of these recipes, as it allows the cooking process, begun under or on the griller, to be continued using very little oil.

My grandmother, Farida Yazbek, with my aunt Susie and kitten, 1922.

Artichoke Soup

1 kg Jerusalem artichokes, scrubbed and diced
2 large onions, diced
1 clove garlic, squashed
2 tablespoons olive oil
3 cups vegetable stock
ground pepper
ground nutmeg

Sweat onions and garlic in oil until shiny. Add artichokes and stir about to sweat for a further 5 minutes. Add stock and simmer until all tender. Purée and serve with a grind of pepper and nutmeg.

Artichoke and Tomato Soup

1 kg Jerusalem artichokes, scrubbed and diced
2 large onions, diced
1 clove garlic, squashed
4 medium tomatoes, diced
2 medium potatoes, diced
2 tablespoons olive oil
3–4 cups vegetable stock
ground pepper
pinch of fresh dill

Sweat onions and garlic in oil until shiny. Add artichokes, tomatoes and potatoes. Sweat further, briefly. Add stock and simmer until all tender. Purée and serve with a grind of pepper and fresh dill.

Broad Bean and Artichoke Bake

If using tinned okra, leave them until last with the artichoke hearts.

1 kg frozen broad beans
500 g fresh okra, left whole
1 tin (410 g) whole artichoke hearts
8 whole Jerusalem artichokes scrubbed and cut in 5 cm chunks
1 large onion, sliced in eighths
2 red capsicum, in thick slices
6 cloves garlic, just squashed
1 tin (410 g) whole peeled tomatoes and juice
1 cup chopped fresh dill
1 teaspoon sweet paprika
1 teaspoon ground cumin
3 bay leaves
2 x 5 cm cassia sticks
375 mL vegetable stock
3 tablespoons olive oil

Put all vegetables in a large roaster or baking dish with a lid and spread the dill and spices over the top. Pour over stock and oil, cover and bake at 200°C for about 35 minutes, stirring once or twice. When all tender, stir through artichokes and rinsed whole okra (if using canned). Return to oven for about 10 more minutes.

Corn and Artichoke Fritters

250 g Jerusalem artichokes, scrubbed and grated
3 cups corn kernels
2 cups besan flour
1 teaspoon baking powder
2 tablespoons chopped parsley
1 tablespoon olive oil
salt
pepper
water
chilli jam, to serve

Mix artichokes and corn. Add remaining ingredients and work to a sticky mixture, adding a tiny bit of water at a time. Bake in little mounds on baking paper at 180°C for about 20 minutes. Serve with chilli jam.

Lemony Artichokes

3 cups diced Jerusalem artichokes, scrubbed
1 tin (410 g) artichoke hearts in brine, rinsed and thinly sliced
1 large onion, sliced in wings
salt
pepper
1 x 3 cm cassia stick
3 or 4 pimento (allspice) berries
80 mL water
60 mL lemon juice
rice, to serve

Sauté onion, diced artichokes and spices in a little oil until they start to glaze. Add water and simmer until tender. Add artichoke hearts and simmer briefly. Add lemon juice and serve with rice.

Mushroom and Artichoke Bake

400 g Jerusalem artichoke, scrubbed and cut to 3 cm pieces
200 g field mushrooms, cut to artichoke size
3 whole cloves garlic
4 slices lemon
ground pepper
3 tablespoons olive oil

Mix all ingredients and bake, uncovered at 190°C, for about 30 minutes.

Olive and Artichoke Salad

400 g Jerusalem artichokes baked and chopped
1 cup capsicum-stuffed green olives, chopped (or 2 tablespoons capers, chopped)
2 tablespoons chopped parsley
ground pepper
2 tablespoons lemon juice
2 tablespoons olive oil
rice, to serve (or pasta)

Mix all ingredients well. May be served on freshly cooked rice or pasta.

Pea and Artichoke Bake

400 g artichokes, scrubbed and cut into egg-size pieces
1 cup peas
2 medium potatoes, quartered
1 onion, quartered
1 tomato, quartered
3 whole cloves garlic
2 tablespoons black olives
1 cup vegetable stock
2 tablespoons olive oil

Mix all ingredients and bake at 190°C for about 50 minutes or until tender.

Tapenade of Artichoke

2 large tinned globe artichoke hearts, drained and chopped
400 g Jerusalem artichokes, roasted, cooled then chopped
2 tablespoons oil
12 green olives, pitted and chopped
1 clove garlic, crushed
50 g light cream cheese
2 tablespoons chopped parsley

Mix ingredients well and season to taste. Serve on canapés.

Plain Fried Eggplant Slices

As a child I hated eggplant, but my grandmother taught me to eat it like this, stabbing at the slices with a corner of fresh Lebanese bread.

1 medium eggplant, peeled and sliced vertically into 1-cm-thick slices
½ cup olive oil
1 lemon

Drop eggplant slices into hot oil and deep-fry until brown on both sides. Serve with a wedge of lemon.

Plain Fried Eggplant Salad

Plain Fried Eggplant Slices
1 or 2 cloves garlic, scored
1 or 2 chillis, chopped
1 tablespoon balsamic vinegar

Layer cooked slices in a shallow bowl, with garlic and chillis in between, sprinkle with balsamic vinegar and serve after 30 minutes.

Eggplant Roulade

Plain Fried Eggplant Slices
filling (see below)
olive oil

Place Plain Fried Eggplant Slices overlapping on a sheet of cling wrap. Spread with filling of choice, roll up and refrigerate in a deepish bowl to catch the oil that will seep off. Serve in slices cut with a knife. The texture will be tender and easy to cut.

Roulade Fillings

Capsicum and Garlic Purée

Can be bottled and refrigerated for a few days.

2 large red capsicum, sliced thinly
1 head of garlic, broken into cloves, unpeeled
1 medium to hot red chilli, left whole
2 tablespoons olive oil
¼ teaspoon salt
¼ teaspoon black pepper
1 tablespoon balsamic vinegar

Place all ingredients in a roasting tin, sprinkle with seasoning and oil and bake for about 40 minutes at 200°C until they begin to brown. Stir though the balsamic vinegar. Cool. Peel the garlic and purée all ingredients.

Cottage Cheese and Thyme

1 cup cottage cheese (or *labne*)
1 tablespoon fresh thyme leaves

Mix together.

Cottage Cheese and Tomato

4 tablespoons semi-dried tomatoes, snipped into small pieces
1 cup cottage cheese (or *labne*)
2 tablespoons chopped fresh mint

Mix together.

Grilled Capsicum

2 large red capsicum, charred over a gas flame

Put into a covered container and when cool, slip off the black skin and slice capsicum thinly.

Red Onion Jam

Delicious, as the vinegar and spices are mildly astringent.

2 red onions, thinly sliced
2 tablespoons oil
3 pimento (allspice) berries
pinch of coriander seeds
1 bay leaf
2 tablespoons brown sugar
1 tablespoon balsamic vinegar

Sauté onions in oil with spices. Add sugar and vinegar and simmer until syrupy.

Grilled Eggplant Salad

These chunks of scored and grilled eggplant are splendid for slow baking in curried or tomatoey sauces. In fact, I now use these grilled pieces in many of my grandmother's recipes, where they used to deep-fry slices, cubes or chunks. It is not necessary to microwave them if they are to be cooked or baked in a sauce. The scoring will assist in the absorption of flavours.

6 medium eggplants
olive oil, to paint
salt
oregano (or rosemary)
lemon, to serve (or lime)

Slice eggplants into 4 vertical pieces, score deeply in a crisscross pattern and skin. Paint with olive oil, sprinkle with salt, oregano/rosemary and place under grill until browned. Remove, place on a microwave tray, and cook on high for 5 minutes or until tender. Serve with wedges of lemon or lime.

EGGPLANT BAKE (MASBAHAT'A DARWISH)

My mother Bertha's recipe for Rosary of the Dervish – I suppose another dish, like Imam Bayildi, suggestive of pleasure-related swooning.

2 medium eggplants, skin on, diced
3 medium onions, cubed
3 medium potatoes, cubed
2 medium carrots, cut into chunks
1 large capsicum, quartered
5 very red tomatoes, quartered
2 bay leaves
ground black pepper
½ teaspoon salt
1 x 5 cm cassia stick
1 heaped teaspoon pimento (allspice)
½ cup water (or stock)
250 g haloumi cheese cut in cubes
4 tablespoons olive oil
rice, to serve
toasted blanched almonds, cashews and pine nuts, to serve (optional)

Mix all ingredients in a covered casserole dish, adding the oil last. Bake for about 50 minutes at 200°C, until tender. Uncover for a few minutes to dry out and crisp the top. A thickish sauce will form in the pan. Serve with rice and, if desired, a sprinkling of the toasted nuts.

EGGPLANT BRAISE (GESMOORDE BRINJAL) WESTERN CAPE STYLE

A quick snack with a fruity chutney.

1 medium eggplant, skin on, diced
1 large onion, sliced
1 tablespoon oil
1 teaspoon chilli, minced
1 teaspoon ground coriander
1 teaspoon ground cumin
1 large carrot, shredded
1 cup peas
salt

Sauté onion in oil. Add spices and stir about. Add vegetables and a few drops of water. Simmer until all tender.

STUFFED EGGPLANT (BUTTENJEN MAHSHI)

Stuffed vegetables are a real specialty of Lebanese cuisine. One can even buy dried, hollowed out eggplants to fill and cook in the winter when fresh ones aren't available. Lebanese or gray zucchini may be used instead of eggplant. In Lebanese cuisine, the lady finger and the tennis ball shapes are the best for stuffing.

12 long lady finger eggplants (or 6 small, bowl-shaped fruit)

Filling

2 tablespoons of chickpeas, soaked overnight, then broken in half
2 tablespoons chopped mint
3 tablespoons chopped parsley
1 large onion, finely chopped
4 medium tomatoes, chopped
1 cup washed Arborio rice
2 tablespoons currants
1 teaspoon salt
1 teaspoon pimento (allspice)
1 teaspoon sumac
pinch of pepper
pinch of cinnamon
2 tablespoons olive oil
3 tablespoons lemon juice
1 fresh tomato
vegetable stock (or water) to cover

Mix the chickpeas with other ingredients. Hollow the eggplants out with a corer, strong zucchini tool, melon baller or sharp knife, and cover the bottom of a saucepan with the insides. Fill hollowed eggplants with vegetables, three quarters to the top, and finish with a tiny cube of fresh tomato. Pack tightly, upright, cover with stock or water and bring to the boil. Simmer until tender, about 45 minutes.

Eggplant Lasagne with Tomato Basil Sauce

I love the light flavours of this eggplant filling.

Lasagne

- 3 cups eggplant, boiled, peeled and mashed
- ½ cup fresh breadcrumbs
- 1 medium sweet onion, finely chopped
- ground pepper
- pinch of dried oregano
- 1 tablespoon parmesan cheese
- 1 tablespoon pine nuts, toasted
- 4 tablespoons basil pesto sauce
- box (250 g) lasagne sheets
- extra parmesan to sprinkle on top
- mixed-leaf salad, to serve

Mix all ingredients, (except lasagne sheets and parmesan for top) together well. Put half a cup of the tomato sauce (below) on the base of a 20 x 20 cm casserole dish. Cover with a lasagne sheet and spread with a couple of spoonsful of the eggplant mixture. Repeat until all of the filling is used, ending with sauce. Sprinkle with parmesan and bake at 190°C for 40 minutes. Serve with a salad of mixed leaves.

Sauce

- 1 bottle (700 g) crushed tomatoes
- 1 tablespoon chopped parsley
- 1 clove garlic, crushed
- ground pepper
- salt
- pinch of sugar
- few torn basil leaves
- dash of olive oil

Blend all ingredients and pour over lasagne, as above.

Loula's Eggplant Omelette

A Greek neighbour in Cape Town, Loula from Lesbos, gave me this recipe.

2 large eggplants, peeled and diced, or prepared as in Grilled Eggplant Salad
1 large onion, chopped
1 clove garlic, chopped
1 tin (410 g) diced tomatoes
4 tablespoons chopped parsley
crumbled feta (or pecorino or mozzarella)
4 eggs

Deep-fry eggplant until sealed, or use grilled chunks. Set aside to drain. Fry onion and garlic in the same emptied pan. Add tomatoes and stew for a few minutes. Place sauce into a casserole dish and lay the eggplant on top. Cover with parsley. Make four depressions, break an egg into each and cover with cheese. Bake at 180°C, until the eggs are set – about 25 minutes.

Eggplant Ragout (Buttenjen Ata)

A vegan dish prepared in Lent by Orthodox Christians in the Middle East. Zucchini or okra may be used instead of eggplant.

4 medium eggplants
1 cup oil
12 small onions, left whole
250 mL tomato purée
1 cup water
salt
pepper
1 teaspoon pimento (allspice)
2 cassia sticks
bunch of coriander, chopped, to serve
60 mL lemon juice, to serve

Peel and cut eggplants into 8 cm pieces and fry in hot oil to seal. Drain. Peel and fry onions in oil, just to seal. Arrange onions and eggplant in a saucepan. Add spices, tomato purée and water. Simmer until all ingredients are tender and the sauce thickens. To finish, add the coriander and lemon juice. Serve warm or cold.

Eggplant Caviar

That smoky-tasting inside of an eggplant grilled whole.

2 medium eggplants

Grill eggplants over a hot flame on the gas burner or barbecue until charred. Put into a suitable bowl and microwave on high for 5 minutes (unless really well done on flame). Split, scoop out flesh, taking care to avoid blackened skin, and dress with either of the fillings below.

Simple Lebanese Caviar

1 cup Eggplant Caviar
sprinkling of salt
3 tablespoons lemon juice
2 tablespoons olive oil
a sprinkling of pimento (allspice)
parsley sprigs, to garnish

Set caviar in a shallow serving bowl, sprinkle with salt, lemon juice and olive oil. Finish with a dash of pimento and a few sprigs of parsley.

Middle Eastern Caviar Salad

A fresh tart taste.

2 cups roughly chopped Eggplant Caviar
4 tablespoons lemon juice
2 tablespoons olive oil
salt
pepper
2 tablespoons chopped parsley
2 tablespoons chopped garlic chives
2 medium, very red tomatoes, finely chopped
1 small red onion, finely chopped
tzatziki, to serve
toasted Arab bread, to serve

Mix all ingredients. Serve with tzatziki, and toasted Arab bread.

EGGPLANT PIES (BOREK)

Makes 4 large pastie-shaped pies. Bottled chilli labne can be purchased from Middle Eastern grocers.

2 sheets puff pastry

Filling

2 cups Eggplant Caviar
4 balls of chilli labne
1 teaspoon dried mint

Mash the filling ingredients together well. Cut 15 cm puff pastry rounds, put half a cup of filling on one side, fold the pastry in a semi-circle over the filling and seal with the other side using a fork. Prick the top and bake at 220°C, until browned. Serve at room temperature.

EGGPLANT CASSEROLE WITH NUTS

This is my take on Sheik 'il Mahshi. It is not necessary to use the variety of nuts – one can simply use almonds. This dish is very rich if the eggplant chunks are first deep-fried to seal in the hot oil and then baked in the sauce.

Eggplant

6 medium eggplants

Slice eggplants in four, lengthwise, score and paint with oil, then grill.

Sauce

1 large onion, sliced in wings
3 cups tomatoes, crushed
pinch of pepper
pinch of sugar
1 teaspoon pimento (allspice)
½ teaspoon cinnamon
2 tablespoons blanched almonds
2 tablespoons pine nuts
3 tablespoons raw cashew pieces
rice, to serve

Sauté onion in a little oil until glazed. Add tomatoes, spices and nuts. Mix well. Remove from heat. Place grilled eggplant chunks in a casserole dish, cover with sauce and bake at 200°C until tender (30–40 minutes). The sauce will reduce while baking and it may be necessary to add a little extra water. Serve hot with rice.

Okra (Bami)

Okra Relish

A warm salad.

2 tablespoons olive oil
250 g okra, chopped
3 cloves garlic
1 medium tomato, quartered
handful of coriander leaves
2 hot chillis, cut in half
4 tablespoons lemon juice

Heat oil, add okra pieces and fry until they develop brown spots. Add garlic, tomatoes, coriander and chillis and stir until just heated through. Finish with lemon juice. Serve at room temperature.

Okra with Potatoes and Amchur

My favourite lunch with a bowl of yoghurt. Amchur *is powdered green mango – available at Indian grocers.*

250 g green okra, sliced lengthwise (or green beans)
4 smallish potatoes, scrubbed and cut into wedges
2 tablespoons flour
2 tablespoons besan flour
salt
pinch of hot chilli powder
½ teaspoon turmeric
1 teaspoon *amchur*
2 tablespoons oil

Mix flours and spices. Toss vegetables in oil to coat and place in baking dish. Cover with spicy flour mixture and stir well to coat. Bake, covered, at 220°C for 25 minutes, and uncovered for a further 15 minutes. Serve warm or at room temperature.

OKRA RAGOUT (BAMI ATA)

In season, my mother made this dish weekly, accompanied by Vermicelli with Rice.

4 cups okra pods, no more than 7 cm long
80 mL oil
1 large onion, sliced in wings
salt
pepper
1 teaspoon pimento (allspice)
2 x 5 cm cassia sticks
250 mL tomato purée
1 cup water
bunch of coriander, chopped
60 mL lemon juice
Vermicelli with Rice, to serve (or bread)

In a medium saucepan, heat oil, drop in okra and fry until they to develop brown spots. Remove to a strainer. Add onions to oil and fry with spices (except coriander). Add tomato purée and water and cook for about 5 minutes. Add okra and coriander and simmer until all ingredients are tender and the sauce thickens. Add lemon juice and serve warm with rice or bread.

OKRA RAGOUT (USING TINNED VEGETABLES)

1 tin (800 g) okra pods, well drained
1 large onion, sliced in wings
2 cloves garlic, crushed
2 tablespoons olive oil
5 tablespoons tomato purée (or 1 cup crushed tomatoes)
2 x 5 cm cassia sticks
1 level teaspoon pimento (allspice) berries
pinch of salt
spinkling of white pepper
pinch of sugar
3 tablespoons chopped coriander leaves
60 mL lemon juice

Sauté onion and garlic in oil with spices. Add tomato and seasonings. Simmer until saucy (a little water may be added with tomato purée). Add okra and boil for 5 minutes, taking care not to break them by harsh stirring. Finish with lemon juice and serve hot or cold.

Tomato Salad with Purslane for Charles

Charles, son of my aunt, Susie, is one of my many cousins in our huge extended family. I grew up on the same block with him and his two sisters, Antoinette and Joanne. The three of us girls tormented him, often to tears. He always stopped crying and swore on his 'Catholic word of honour' not to tell when I promised to make him a dish of his all-time favourite tomato salad. It was this salad that made him promise, when we were about eight years old, to marry me one day, although he would never allow me to kiss him until then!

6 medium, very red tomatoes, finely chopped
1 small sweet onion, finely chopped
1 clove garlic, crushed
4 tablespoons chopped parsley
4 cups purslane leaves
3 tablespoons lemon juice
3 tablespoons olive oil
salt
ground black pepper

Toss ingredients together and stand for a few minutes before serving.

Tomato Slices with Spicy Juices

A great breakfast dish with Turkish toast.

3 large, very red tomatoes, in 3-cm-thick slices
1 tablespoon olive oil
pinch of salt
pinch of black pepper
pinch of pimento (allspice)

Place slices in a single layer in an ovenproof dish, sprinkle with oil and spices and place under the grill for about 5 minutes, on each side.

ZUCCHINI BITES (KOUSA B'BEID)

3 large zucchini, grated
1 large onion, grated
1 large handful of parsley, chopped
1 small handful of oregano, chopped
pinch of salt
pinch of ground pepper
1 teaspoon baking powder
4 tablespoons flour
1 egg

Blend all ingredients and stand for 30 minutes. Stir thoroughly again. Bake small mounds or flat, saucer-size shapes on baking tray (oiled or covered with baking paper) at 200°C for 15 minutes.

ZUCCHINI OMELETTE (M'FARKIE)

As a child I hated this dish, and now I can't get enough of it.

2 medium-size black, green or grey zucchini, coarsely grated
1 medium onion, finely chopped
1 tablespoon oil
1 medium tomato, cubed
1 tablespoon chopped mint
1 tablespoon chopped parsley
pinch of pimento (allspice)
salt
pepper
4 eggs, beaten
1 lemon, wedged, to serve

Heat oil and sauté onion. Add the tomato, grated zucchini and herbs, cook on medium heat until almost done, then stir in spices and pour eggs over. Stir now and again until set. Serve with lemon wedges.

STUFFED ZUCCHINI (KOOSA MAHSHI)

12 grey zucchini
3 pimento (allspice) berries
1 x 3 cm cassia stick

Filling

2 tablespoons chickpeas, soaked overnight, then broken in half
2 tablespoons chopped mint
3 tablespoons chopped parsley
1 large onion, finely chopped
4 medium tomatoes, chopped
1 cup basmati rice, washed
2 tablespoons currants
1 teaspoon salt
1 teaspoon pimento (allspice)
1 teaspoon sumac
pinch of pepper
2 tablespoons olive oil
3 tablespoons lemon juice
1 fresh tomato, cubed

Mix filling ingredients. Hollow zucchini and place in the bottom of a saucepan with all the spices. Fill hollowed zucchinis with vegetables, three quarters to the top, and finish with a tiny cube of fresh tomato. Pack tightly, upright, add the pimento berries and cassia stick, cover with stock or water and bring to the boil. Simmer until tender, about 45 minutes. Leave to settle in the pot for about 15 minutes before serving, as they may break.

Zucchini with Ricotta Topping

Base

3 medium zucchini, sliced
1 medium carrot, sliced
1 medium onion, chopped
1 bay leaf
1 tablespoon oil
1 tin (410 g) diced tomatoes and juice
salt
black pepper

Topping

1 cup ricotta cheese
2 teaspoons flour
1 egg
2 tablespoons chopped parsley
pinch of dried thyme
pinch of oregano
salt
black pepper

Fry the onion and bay leaf in oil, add carrots and zucchini and after 5 minutes, add tomatoes and seasoning. Tip all into a baking dish. Beat all topping ingredients together well and pour over the vegetables. Bake uncovered at 190°C for about 35 minutes, until set.

Let the stranger in your midst be to you
as the native for you were strangers
in the land of Egypt.

– Jewish saying

The Continuing Gift of my Jewish Christmas

One night, some time back, my adult son rang me. It was later than usual – everyone knows I'm an early bird – but he was elated and wanted to tell me of his evening out. Sleepy mother, I listened patiently and then asked if we could continue the conversation the next day, when my eyes would be open.

Myself and my sister, Michele, a pair of Christmas angels, 1958.

Every year since I left home as a teenager, I've had a partially Jewish Christmas, with close friends and family gathering on the day. Some years it has been a totally Jewish affair: it is, after all, the birthday of a wayward Jewish boy!

One Christmas, my friend Charmaine consulted me about who to invite and where we'd have the lunch – her place or mine – and we agreed she had more space. 'I've met this couple,' she said, 'asylum seekers, quite young, so tragic – been tortured, jailed, just trying to become "normal" as they await visas.'

'Of course you must ask them,' I said. 'Yes, please do.'

So we sat to lunch on 25 December – twelve of us, disparate as always but with a common intention to relax, enjoy the meal and chat. The twelve different desserts that covered the table could have satisfied 144 people. Hamid and Samira (not their real names), with colouring similar to mine and looking like our family, participated wholeheartedly. My son sat at their end of the table and soon phone numbers were exchanged. Within a week, a dinner date was set.

With motherly interference I reminded my son that he was to pay; no way on a Red Cross stipend could they afford even a normal meal for themselves. Hamid and Samira are both quite skinny, showing lack of money and too much stress. Before the dinner, the couple went to Charmaine's work to tell her they'd be meeting my son. It was after that dinner that my son rang me.

The couple must have enjoyed their Thai meal, because the next day they turned up once more at Charmaine's work to say just that. Meanwhile, in our continuing conversation, my son enthused about this talented pair and how they inspired him. Despite their unknown fate and all they had been through, their visa status holding them in limbo, their vitality was intact. At one stage, in the restaurant, Hamid began to speak of the torture that smashed his limbs, but Samira said to stop. When my son asked them about others he knew of from their country, he noticed that their faces shut down. I explained that in countries with an active secret police service, people no longer trusted one another, as they feared being spied on.

My son, disillusioned with middle-class, materialistic values, was showing compassion and concern for those desperate for an opportunity to live, work and breathe in a fair society.

'I'm going away,' he told them. 'But as soon as I return, I'll call you and we can go out again.'

'Yes, but we pay,' they said.

'Don't worry about that now. Let's just go out for a feed and a yarn,' he replied.

Despite the fact that some of our histories are trammelled by ethnicity, my son is discovering our common humanity in a world of hyphenated identity, and my joy in his discovery is the continuing gift of that particular Jewish Christmas.

A Little South African Background

In the seventeenth century, the Dutch East India Trading Company started a market garden at the Cape of Good Hope, on the southernmost tip of Africa, to supply vessels sailing between Europe and the Far East. As the settlement grew, the indigenous population felt threatened. Soldiers were brought from Europe – among them mercenaries from Germany, Holland and Sweden to guard the gardens. Slaves were brought from Batavia (Java and Sumatra) in the eighteenth century to work the garden. The Malays, as the Batavian slaves were called, were Muslim and ate halal food. Among them there were many skilled tradesmen: tilers and stonemasons who worked on the construction of some of the earliest buildings in what was to become Cape Town. They settled in the Western Cape where they live in enclaves like the Bo-kaap, still celebrating their religious festivals and preparing food in the Malay style.

Mr Fataar was the Malay vendor whose veggie truck came by our home every week, many years ago in Cape Town. He'd drive into the suburbs and park for a couple of hours. His little assistant came to the door with a sample basket and the housekeeper would give him a list. Usually, though, I'd go out to the truck and we'd have a long chat accompanied by tea and cake.

He paid me the ultimate compliment one day when he said that as he drove down my street, the smell of garlic and spices cooking made him think a *haji* lived there. A *haji* is a devotee who'd made the pilgrimage to Mecca and cooked delicious meals, he told me, for her family.

In 1820 the British set up a colonial service with hundreds of settlers to run the Cape Colony and Natal. They also brought Indians as indentured labourers to cultivate and harvest the sugar cane in Natal. Indian cuisine had a strong influence all over the country. In 1867, diamonds were discovered and in 1886, gold was found and people hurried there from all over the world. Jews fleeing Cossack pogroms in Eastern Europe and a few Lebanese, some of my ancestors fleeing Ottoman sorrow makers, sailed down the east coast of Africa and moved into Southern Africa. After settling their families, the men set off with wagons and carts, plying their trade as hawkers selling household and farm goods in rural areas.

Malays and Indians, as local people, became cooks and domestic workers in more affluent households, the food of Europe was spiced up: a simple stew would have ginger, garlic and chillis added; puddings were rich, reflecting the Dutch taste for butter and cream, with cinnamon, nutmeg and other spices from the east.

Traditional tribes, among them Xhosa and Zulu, grew corn and herded cattle. Many of us fondly recall giant pots of corn porridge or cracked corn with beans shared with our nursemaids. Growing up, I saw African people, no matter how poor, share whatever they were about to consume. A box of cigarettes, or even a hand-rolled, brown-paper *zol*, was passed along a queue at a bus stop; no one even wondered where it had come from – it belonged to everyone waiting.

Wherever we are in the world, our celebrations are coloured by both our history as well as the culture in which we live.

I've often mused on how we in Australia celebrate Christmas (the birth of a child more than 2000 years ago, a child that would later take a stand for the poor) by rushing out to kill and eat anything that walks, swims or flies. It seems to be a time of excess noise, food and spending of both money and energy. A little zen reminder for this time: 'Carry one thing with two hands rather than two things with one hand.'

Lebanese bathing beauties – 1940, East London.

And here I find myself carrying two things in each hand – diverse aspects of Christmas for my brindle children, their Afrikaans and Mediterranean heritages represented in this selection. Afrikaans cooking of the Western Cape, including all the salads, pickles and *boboties*, reveal Creole-type sweet and sour flavours, floridly displaying Malay, Indian and Dutch influences.

The Mediterranean recipes, in the second part of the chapter, are drawn from Lebanese, Greek and my daughter's favourite Southern European and

North African foods. The eggplant roulade in this festive menu contains a rich capsicum, walnut and caper filling. In all of these rather exuberant recipes, I have cooked for colour and appearance while striving for menu coherence in the multitude of flavours.

Those musical Sanans in 1930s East London.

SWEET 'N' SOUR CUCUMBERS TRADITIONAL SOUTH AFRICAN STYLE

Delectable colours on a festive table.

3 large continental cucumbers in 1-cm-thick slices, skin on
3 tablespoons salt
4 medium onions, sliced in rings
1 green pepper, chopped
1 red pepper, chopped
1 L white vinegar
1 dessertspoon celery seed
1 teaspoon turmeric
1 teaspoon mustard seed
1 cup raw sugar

Slice cucumbers, sprinkle with salt, and leave to drain in a colander for 4 hours. Rinse cucumbers. Put the vinegar, spices and sugar into saucepan and dissolve on a moderate heat. Add vegetables, bring to the boil for 2 minutes. Bottle and seal while hot. When cool, refrigerate and serve with drinks at room temperature.

TAMARI NUTS TO SERVE WITH DRINKS

Any combination of nuts can be used here: almonds, cashews, macadamias, but toast separately in a dry pan or microwave. Sesame and sunflower seeds are good as part of a mix, as they clump together.

375 g pepitas, toasted slowly in a dry pan
1 teaspoon tamari (or soya sauce)
1 teaspoon honey
pinch of hot chilli
¼ teaspoon ground coriander
less than a teaspoon of sesame oil

Mix all dressing ingredients to moisten nuts and keep stirring in a dry pan over heat until crisp and dry. If the bottom of the pan starts to burn, put everything into a shallow dish and microwave for about 5 minutes, until crisp and dry, tossing after each minute, or toast in conventional oven at 200°C until crisp.

Beetroot Soup

This recipe is always found at Christmas in South Africa. The colour of this soup enhances a festive table – whatever one is celebrating. Here's my take on this Eastern European favourite.

2 medium beetroots
1 vegetable stock cube
750 mL water
1 bay leaf
2 medium potatoes
2 medium carrots
1 large onion
1 teaspoon salt
sour cream, to serve (or yoghurt)
chopped chives, to serve

Peel and dice the beetroots and add to a medium saucepan with stock cube, water and bay. Boil for about 30 minutes until barely tender. Add peeled and diced potato, carrot and onion and simmer for about 15 minutes until tender. Adjust seasoning. Add more water if necessary. Serve hot or chilled with a dollop of sour cream/ yoghurt and a generous spoonful of finely chopped chives.

Bobotie

Bobotie, Afrikaans, is a baked spicy loaf usually topped with a custard of two eggs beaten with a cup of milk and baked until set.

If using the custard, cook the loaf for ten minutes less than suggested, decorate the top with almonds and bay or lemon leaves, pour the custard over and return to the oven until set.

Choose one of these recipes for a special occasion. They each serve eight with rice and side dishes.

Bobotie with Beans

1 large onion, diced
3 tablespoons olive oil
1 tablespoon fragrant curry powder
4 tablespoons cider vinegar
4 tablespoons water
2 tablespoons fruit chutney
2 cups cooked brown beans, minced
2 cups cooked brown beans, left whole
1 large carrot, coarsely shredded
½ cup cashew pieces
1 tablespoon soya sauce
½ cup plumped sultanas
2 tablespoons blanched almonds
6 bay leaves
rice and salad, to serve

To plump sultanas, put into a microwave bowl with half a cup of water and boil for a minute. Set aside. In a large saucepan, sauté onion in oil. When just softening, add curry powder and stir. Then add vinegar, water and chutney. Mix. Add the remaining ingredients and pour into a casserole dish (approximately 20 x 25 cm). Stud the top with blanched whole almonds or sunflower seeds and bay leaves. Bake at 180°C for 30–40 minutes. Serve with steamed rice or Yellow Rice with Raisins and salad.

Bobotie with Nuts

2 medium onions, chopped
2 tablespoons oil
1 tablespoon fragrant curry powder
2 cups nuts, finely chopped
1 cup soft brown breadcrumbs
2 medium carrots, grated
1 tablespoon fruit chutney
2 tablespoons raisins (or sultanas)
2 tablespoons cider vinegar
1 teaspoon turmeric
1 vegetable stock cube, in 1 cup hot water
2 tablespoons blanched almonds
6 bay leaves
rice and salad, to serve

In a large saucepan, sauté onion in oil. When just softening, add curry powder and stir. Add the remaining ingredients. Pack into an oiled oven-proof dish, decorate with bay leaves and a few blanched almonds and bake at 180°C for about 30 minutes. Serve with rice and salad.

Bobotie with Carrots

1 large onion, chopped
2 tablespoons oil
1 tablespoon curry powder
3 tablespoons cider vinegar
1 large tomato, chopped
1 tablespoon turmeric
pinch of ground ginger
½ cup sultanas
1 cup mushrooms, sliced
2 cups brown breadcrumbs
1 cup nuts, ground
6 cups carrots, grated
½ vegetable stock cube in ½ cup boiling water
6 dried apricots, chopped
½ cup blanched almonds
6 bay leaves
rice and salad, to serve

In a large saucepan, sauté onion in oil. When just softening, add curry powder and stir. Add vinegar and tomato, then the rest of the ingredients, except for the almonds and bay leaves. Mix well and pack into a casserole dish. Decorate the top with the almonds and bay leaves. Bake at 180°C for 45 minutes.

Salads

These traditional recipes were handed down through generations of Afrikaaner families in the Western Cape of South Africa. Because of the vinegar, they keep well for some weeks, covered, in the fridge.

CURRIED BEAN SALAD (INGELEGDE GROENBOONTJIES)

500 g green beans, chopped
250 g onions, chopped
salt
1 cup water
2 tablespoons raw sugar
2 teaspoons curry powder
1 teaspoon turmeric
180 mL cider vinegar
1 heaped tablespoon cornflour

Bring the beans, onions, salt and water to the boil and simmer for about 10 minutes, until the beans and onions are just tender. Add sugar, stir to dissolve. Add curry powder and turmeric. Stir well. Simmer. Add cornflour to vinegar, stir well and add to boiling beans. Stir while boiling until clear. Bottle and seal while hot. Refrigerate once cooled. Will keep for up to one month.

SAUCY BEAN SALAD (SOUSBOONTJIES)

2 cups kidney beans, soaked overnight
1 teaspoon salt
pepper
2 tablespoons raw sugar
1 tablespoon flour
80 mL cider vinegar

Boil beans for about 40 minutes, until tender. Add salt, pepper and sugar. Slake flour with vinegar and add to the bean mixture to thicken. Serve warm or cold. Store in a covered container in the fridge for up to a month.

Cucumber Cooler

A lovely refresher with a spicy meal.

4 Lebanese cucumbers, peeled and grated
1 tablespoon salt
2 tablespoons cider vinegar
pinch of sugar
1 mild green chilli, chopped

Salt cucumber and leave to drain. Rinse and pat dry. Dress with vinegar, sugar and chilli.

Eggplant Pickle Salad

This unusual dish mimics the pickled fish of the Western Cape people in South Africa. It keeps well in the fridge and is a splendid lunch dish with potatoes or bread to slurp up the sauce.

2 large eggplants
olive oil, to paint

Slice eggplants into thick semi-circles, paint with oil and place under the grill. Turn over when browned. Finish cooking in microwave, if desired.

Sauce

3 tablespoons oil
10 cloves
10 pimento (allspice) berries
1 dried red chilli, cut in 3
4 large onions, sliced into rings
1 tablespoon raw sugar
1 teaspoon turmeric
1 teaspoon curry powder
2 teaspoons ground coriander
½ cup cider vinegar
1 cup water
3 bay leaves

Heat oil and fry cloves, pimento berries and chilli. Add onions and fry briefly. Sprinkle this mixture with sugar, turmeric, curry powder and coriander. Stir to coat. Add vinegar, water and bay leaves and simmer for about 5 minutes. Pour hot sauce over the eggplant, shake through and allow to stand overnight. Serve cold.

Onions in Mustard Sauce (Uiwe in Mosterd Sous)

An old recipe from a Cape Dutch kitchen.

3 large eggs
1 teaspoon powdered mustard
pinch of salt
½ cup white sugar
1 cup cider vinegar
½ cup water
500 g small onions, lightly boiled
(or 500 g blanched green beans, or a mixture of both)

Beat eggs, mustard, salt and sugar for about 5 minutes. Add vinegar and water and beat again for 1–2 minutes. Stir slowly over a low heat in a double boiler until it coats the back of a spoon, taking care not to allow the sauce to curdle or separate. Pour warm sauce over well-drained vegetables. Cool. This salad will keep for up to 1 week, stored covered in the refrigerator.

Yellow Rice with Raisins (Geelrys met Rosyntjies)

Usually served on Sundays in South Africa.

2 cups basmati rice, well washed
1 tablespoon oil
¼ teaspoon salt
½ cup raisins
1 teaspoon turmeric
4 cloves
6 snipped cardamom pods
3 x 3 cm cinnamon sticks
4 cups water

Put all ingredients into a saucepan, bring to the boil and cook on very low until all liquid is absorbed. Just before serving, fork through to spread colour evenly.

Mediterranean Mezze

Here is a selection of festive fingerfood from Africa to Asia, with a taste of Italy in-between.

Harissa with Beetroot

Beetroot enhances the colour and deepens the flavour of this traditional mezze *dish from North Africa.*

1 red capsicum, roasted, skinned and deveined
1 cup medium to hot chillies, chopped
8 cloves garlic
pinch of hot chilli flakes
1 teaspoon caraway seeds
2 teaspoons ground coriander
1 teaspoon ground cumin
½ cup fresh mint leaves
1 tablespoon balsamic vinegar
pinch of salt
little oil
1 tin (410 g) beetroot, drained

Put all ingredients, except beetroot, into the bowl of a food processor and mill to a saucy consistency. Add beetroot and process again until chunky.

Tapenade for Feasting

2 cups Kalamata olives, pitted
1 cup capsicum-stuffed green olives
6 halves of sun-dried tomatoes (no oil), finely diced
1 tablespoon small capers
2 teaspoons Pickled Lemons, roughly chopped
2 tablespoons olive oil
2 tablespoons pomegranate molasses
pinch of hot chilli flakes
½ teaspoon fennel seeds, lightly toasted
pinch of dried oregano
ground black pepper
melba toasts, to serve

Put all ingredients into the bowl of a food processor and mill to a chunky consistency. Serve with melba toasts. The rest may be bottled and stored in the fridge for some weeks, or frozen in usable quantities.

Chickpea Balls with Aglione Flavours

Ines and Emmie gave me the recipe for this seasoning from their aunt in Bologna.

1 tin (410 g) chickpeas, rinsed and drained
2 bay leaves
2 tablespoons chopped fresh rosemary
3 fresh sage leaves, finely chopped
1 clove garlic, crushed
pinch of hot chilli
pinch of salt
pinch of ground pepper
2 tablespoons sun-dried tomatoes, finely chopped

Bring chickpeas to the boil with 2 bay leaves and cook for 3 minutes, just to heat through. Drain, remove bay leaves and transfer to a food processor with the rest of the ingredients. Mill to a smoothish paste. When cool enough to handle, roll into bite-size balls and chill.

Mushroom Patties with Dipping Sauce

My daughter's version of Antonio Carluccio's mushroom rissoles.

Patties

2 cups mushroom pieces, grilled
1 tablespoon red onion, finely chopped
1 cup fresh breadcrumbs
2 eggs, beaten
2 teaspoons baby capers
2 tablespoons toasted pine nuts
pinch of salt
ground black pepper

Squash all together, adding more breadcrumbs if too wet. Put golf-ball size mounds on an oven tray lined with baking paper and bake at 200°C for about 20 minutes.

Sauce

1 clove garlic
pinch of salt
black pepper
small bunch of basil
2 teaspoons lemon juice
2 tablespoons olive oil

Put garlic with salt and pepper into the bowl of a food processor and mill to a chunky consistency. Add basil and mill until finely processed. Add oil and lemon, blend well and use as a dip for mushroom patties.

EGGPLANT ROULADE WITH WALNUT AND CAPSICUM FILLING

A Mediterranean feast would be incomplete without an eggplant dish, a pilaff and something stuffed …

Roulade

Eggplant Roulade to serve 6 people

Filling

1 clove garlic, little salt
1 red capsicum, roasted
1 cup walnuts, washed
1 tablespoon pomegranate molasses
1 tablespoon tiny capers

Process garlic and salt. Add the rest of the ingredients, except capers and mill to a chunky consistency. Fold in the capers. Use the filling to prepare Eggplant Roulade.

PERSIAN PILAFF WITH BARBERRIES

Rice sprinkled with gold and rubies – a royal dish.

3 tablespoons olive oil
½ cup barberries (*zereshk*), washed
½ cup flaked almonds
3 cups basmati rice, cooked
few strands saffron in 2 tablespoons water
sumac, to sprinkle
½ cup carrot, coarsely grated, blanched in boiling water and drained
tarragon, to garnish (or mint leaves)

Heat oil and fry barberries and almonds. Sprinkle soaked saffron over hot rice, then pour barberries, nuts and carrot over. Fork through, sprinkle with sumac, garnish with tarragon or mint leaves and serve immediately.

Vegetable Pies

These little pizzas are lovely as a starter with drinks – they have a Syrian connection. Use Oil Pastry, bread dough or three sheets of ready-rolled puff pastry to make mini-pizza bases.

1 large onion, sliced
½ teaspoon fenugreek seeds
2 tablespoons oil
2 medium green peppers, seeded and chopped
2 medium red peppers, seeded and chopped
2 tablespoons chopped parsley
pinch of cinnamon
pinch of pimento (allspice)
2 tablespoons walnut pieces
4 tablespoons lemon juice
1 level teaspoon sumac
pinch of salt
sprinkle of white pepper

Sauté seeds and onion in oil. Add peppers and continue cooking until soft. Add remaining ingredients and mix well. Form rounds of Oil Pastry or bread dough and place a generous amount of the mixture on top. Bake at 200°C until browned – approximately 20 minutes.

Tzatziki with Feta

An Egyptian version.

2 cups Greek-style yoghurt
½ cup feta cheese, crumbled
ground pepper
1 clove garlic, crushed
1 tablespoon white wine vinegar
1 tablespoon olive oil

Blend all ingredients in a food processor.

STUFFED TOMATOES (BANNADOORA MAHSHI)

Served alongside Tzatziki with Feta, these are shiny Christmas baubles waiting to be eaten!

Tomatoes

24 plum-size tomatoes

Cut a thin slice off the bottom of the tomato and reserve the slice for covering. Scoop out the insides of the tomato, using a melon baller, and keep to use in the filling, squeezing out some of the seeds, if possible.

Stuffing

insides of tomatoes, some seeds removed
2 tablespoons pine nuts
2 tablespoons chopped mint
3 tablespoons chopped parsley
1 large onion, finely chopped
1 cup washed Arborio rice
2 tablespoons currants
1 teaspoon salt
1 teaspoon pimento (allspice)
1 teaspoon sumac
pinch of pepper
pinch of cinnamon
2 tablespoons lemon juice
2 tablespoons olive oil
150 mL boiling water
2 tablespoons oil

Mix all the ingredients well except boiling water and 2 tablespoons olive oil. Fill tomatoes not quite to the top, and place close together in a roasting tin. Pour over 2 tablespoons oil and about 150 mL boiling water. Cover each tomato with reserved slice and bake at 200°C for about 45 minutes. Leave to cool in pan.

Lebanese Lore

I feel a recipe is only a theme,
which an intelligent cook can play
each time with a variation.

– Madame Benoit

Bittersweet Moments

Every year, just before her September birthday, my daughter leaves home to return to university. She is away for nine months. 'I could have a baby,' she teases me, 'and you wouldn't even know!'

Once she arrives at her destination, we have our first chat: 'How was the flight? How's the weather? Have you eaten yet? What did you eat?' Questions tumble out of me as I try to remain part of her life. I was a student once, but I never lived and studied alone overseas. Then I fill her in on how cold or windy it still is (she's been gone twenty-four hours) and whether the dog is pining for her.

The days pass cleaning the house, sorting out the spring garden and always writing something. There's not much cooking. Alone, I prefer fruit or a few steamed vegetables, and I hear my gourmet daughter's enthusiasm, as she seeks out the best olives, garlic, artichokes and chilli for her dinner. I cannot deny that she learnt to cook at home with me – participatory learning, without the pedantry that I experienced with my grandmother.

When she was a young teenager, I went through a phase of swooning in the kitchen! Unlike the apocryphal Turkish imam who swooned after eating that eggplant dish, I'd most likely been overdoing things. It happened sometimes when I prepared dinner; she would help me to a seat, give me a glass of water and resume the interrupted process of a recipe that was taking shape out of my own head. Our cooking together grew into regular weekend feasts and was probably fuelled by my subconscious memories of being initiated and guided into the mysteries and pleasures of kitchen hours by Granny Isabel. Granny's comforting hands soothed her grandchildren, while her interest in teaching us our traditional foods relieved her sense of exile in South Africa. Like my grandmother who lived overseas and away from her family, my overseas daughter adds inventiveness to what she has learnt, preparing feasts that delight her colleagues and friends, and comfort her while she is far from home.

Christmas comes and goes with cracked voices on the telephone. Weeks turn into months and, as my birthday looms, I realise she'll be home. The week before she arrives, our phone calls are speedy.

'Have you packed?'

'Mum,' she labours, 'I have a huge paper to present before I can even think about travelling.'

'But you're coming home,' I sing.

And then, twenty-four hours before she arrives, almost like the time she was born, I become quiet. I sit in my garden and watch the sky, birds flitting and aeroplanes sailing. It's the sea, I always told my children: planes glide on waves, currents and tides, just like ships. My expectant heart's low hum accompanies my breath, praying for safe passage once more.

The coming and going of my child is an inward, intensely personal journey. In my joy at her arrival are the seeds of her eventual departure – a holiday with bittersweet moments for both of us. Nonetheless, our love of food and cooking is not muted as each day we pursue flavours and ingredients in all quarters of the city. We both laugh at the memory of a Sunday lunch in a south Indian restaurant, when a man leant across to where we sat encircled by bowls and platters.

'You'll need a man to help you finish that.'

'Watch us,' my daughter replied.

And he did, staring all the way to the last bare bowl.

She triumphantly regales my friends with the story of my lust in Haberfield, when she had to help me out of the Italian place because I ate so much.

Two weeks before she leaves, we talk about how tired we feel.

'Bone-weary,' I say.

'Whacked,' she says.

I marvel at her capacity, despite her own sadness about leaving her elderly dog and the safety of home, to return to those challenges – an adventurer, a friend once called her.

Our conversation starts to diverge. We tell each other what we will be doing and indirectly, how we hope to be. Once she is there and settled, we will resume our food and recipe conversations as we describe to each other what we have cooked or are cooking and with whom we will share it.

The day she prepares to board that aeroplane, my heart aches at our separation. But my joy is much larger, as she has the freedom to pursue her passion for study in a field that acknowledges her excellence.

Go, daughter, fly, sail on wings of delight in life that daily, wherever you are, offers you its bounty.

Wholeheartedly, I remain behind.

Stories From Long Ago

Lebanon sits on the edge of the eastern Mediterranean coast. It is bordered by Syria and Israel. The population is made up of Christian (among them, Orthodox and Maronite Catholic), Druze and Muslim – both Sunni and Shi'a.

In the nineteenth century, Jesuit priests planted vineyards in the Bekaa Valley – winemaking has continued to this day. However, *arak*, the anise-flavoured liqueur, similar to Greek ouzo, remains the most popular drink. Alcohol is always served with food.

Despite the small area of the country, there are regional variations in the spicing and content of most recipes. As with most Mediterranean diets, there is an emphasis on fruit and vegetables, seeds and nuts, breads and, of course, some animal products. It is a cuisine renowned for its blend of Western and oriental flavours. *Burghul* (boiled, dried and cracked wheat) is an important ingredient in Lebanese dishes – *tabbouleh* and *kibbe* being most notable.

My granny, Isabel, the one who taught me to cook, smoking nhargile with her sister, Eva, in Lebanon, 1956.

My mother, Bertha, and my grandmother, Isabel, were pedantic cooks. Only the cooking of their region of Lebanon was acceptable. All the rest was rubbish and adulterated. So my father's sisters, who put mint in the *kibbe* or tomato in their vine leaves, were not part of this orthodox cooking conversation. However, in my opinion, authenticity of dishes is a moot point among such widely dispersed Lebanese communities; what is more important is what suits one's palate and the ingredients and menu at hand. Of all Lebanese cooks, my mother stood alone on the question of garlic: she hated the smell on the breath or in the food and said it labelled us as different and had set her apart when she was at school.

In the early days of Lebanese migration to South Africa, there were no basic Middle Eastern foodstuffs available for purchase until my grandfather's Queenstown business, Haddad Brothers, began importing. When he died, my grandmother and mother had to make all their own basics from scratch. For *za'ater*, sumac was only imported much later, so they relied on migrants bringing quantities to share around, but in the meantime they used a mix of dried oregano, sesame seeds and salt, adding lemon juice and oil. Lemon appears in almost every salad, many other dishes and, certainly, in all cabbage and cauliflower dishes. This is not to everyone's taste: Northern Italian palates find some of our food too sharp and spicy.

I remember how Granny and my mother made *burghul* and *kishk* in the back garden; they dried the boiled wheat in the sun on long tables covered with sheets. Later, Haddads, who farmed cherries and wheat near the Lesotho border, made *burghul* and *kishk* for delivery all over the country.

When I set up my home in Cape Town, I made my own yoghurt, which I put into a muslin bag and hung on the clothes line, in the shade, for a few hours to make *labne.* When I moved to Sydney, I tried the same thing. Imagine my shock when, a few hours later I found what looked like tufts of fluff hanging in the trees and dotted on the ground. The muslin bag was hanging on the line like a shredded breast. Manna from heaven, the magpies and currawongs must have thought when they attacked the makings of my dinner.

So it is that cooking from my ancestral tradition, I am never alone in the kitchen, my mother and grandmothers hover as I develop a recipe beyond what they taught me. The questions and requests of my guests and cooking students echo in my head, leading my knife and spoon into shaping a dish for their tastes. As I blend my ideas with their preferences, cooking becomes an intimate process.

Looking deeply into my saucepans, I see the faces of my friends and, mindful of their likes and dislikes, I increase or reduce the chilli, garlic and spices.

My parents visiting with Yazbek cousins in the Cedars, Lebanon, 1965.

Salad

A selection of traditional styles with my own variations, these salads are unusual and some, like *Burghul* Salad, quite substantial in themselves. Any of these can be part of a *mezze* feast.

Cauliflower with Lemon (Arnabeet b'Hamoud)

Instead of deep-frying, this method works well.

4 tablespoons olive oil
5 cups chopped cauliflower
juice of 1 lemon
juice of 1 lime

Heat oil until smoking and drop dry florets in. Cover and cook on high, stirring from time to time. It takes about 12 minutes. Add juices and pour all into serving bowl for *mezze*.

Burghul Salad

Not tabbouleh*!*

1 cup *burghul*, soaked and squeezed
6 medium tomatoes, finely chopped
1 sweet onion, finely chopped
1 teaspoon chopped fresh marjoram
1 tablespoon chopped fresh oregano
2 tablespoons chopped fresh basil
2 tablespoons chopped fresh mint
1 small hot chilli, seeded and chopped
½ teaspoon salt
pinch of white pepper
pinch of pimento (allspice)
pinch of cinnamon
2 tablespoons olive oil

Mix all ingredients well and chill.

Cabbage Pilaff with Burghul

Delicious with yoghurt.

1 large onion, diced
3 tablespoons olive oil
½ savoy cabbage, finely shredded
½ cup coarse *burghul*, washed and left to stand
½ teaspoon salt
a generous sprinkling of white pepper
little water

Heat oil in a saucepan and fry onions until beginning to colour. Add the cabbage and stir about. Cover and allow to soften on a moderate heat. Add *burghul* and seasoning. Cover and allow to swell over low heat, adding a few drops of water from time to time if necessary.

Cabbage Salad with Lemon

A very lemony salad to serve with kibbe.

8 cups finely shredded red or white cabbage
1 teaspoon salt
150 mL lemon juice
2 tablespoons olive oil

Put sliced cabbage into a large bowl, sprinkle with salt and bruise, rubbing and squeezing. This will release sugars from the stalks. Add lemon and oil, stir and chill before serving.

Beetroot with Tahini

boiled baby beetroots, whole (or large beetroots, sliced)
beetroot stalks and leaves, chopped and steamed or boiled
2 tablespoons tahini
1 clove garlic, crushed
60 mL lemon juice
pinch of salt
water

Process tahini, garlic, lemon and salt with enough water to make a creamy sauce. Dress the cooked stalks, leaves and beetroots while warm, and serve at room temperature.

Cucumber in Yoghurt, with Mint

500 g Greek-style yoghurt
3 Lebanese cucumbers, thinly sliced
salt
½ cup fresh mint, chopped
(or 1 teaspoon dried)

Mix ingredients and serve.

Green Beans with Caramelised Onions (Luby b'zeit)

This dish takes an hour or more to cook, so I make a lot at once.

1 kg green beans
3 onions, sliced in wings
5 tablespoons olive oil
8 cloves garlic, crushed
1 tin (410 g) whole peeled tomatoes
½ teaspoon salt
shake of white pepper
bread, to serve

Heat oil and fry onions until very brown. Add beans on high heat and shake the pot. Do this 3 or 4 times. Add garlic and tomatoes. Reduce heat and simmer for up to 60 minutes until all the ingredients have collapsed. No water is added. Serve at room temperature with good bread to soak the juices.

Green Salad with Haloumi Cheese

1 cup haloumi cheese, diced and grilled
large bunch of continental parsley,
finely chopped
small bunch of fresh mint, finely chopped
12 shallots, sliced
2 Lebanese cucumbers, finely diced
juice of 1 lemon
1 tablespoon olive oil
1 teaspoon sumac

Mix all ingredients, except the cheese and sumac. Top with cheese and sprinkle with sumac.

The word *kibbe* literally translates as 'paste'. The glory of Lebanese cuisine, it is made of *burghul* with spices and either a flesh or vegetable binder. In Lent, pumpkins and potatoes are the most popular varieties.

Kibbe Noodles

2 cups fine *burghul*, washed, soaked for 30 minutes, then drained and squeezed
1 large onion, minced
1 cup flour
1 teaspoon salt
1 teaspoon pepper
1 teaspoon ground cumin

Make dough with the *burghul*, flour, onion and spices. Knead thoroughly and pinch off marble-size balls. Flatten on the palm of your hand to make a shell. Place in a single layer on a floured board. Bring a large deep saucepan of water to the boil. Drop noodles in and boil for 10 minutes or until tender, but not falling apart. Serve with a pasta sauce or strewn through a platter of fried onions with cooked spinach tossed through.

Kibbe Paté

Serve with a tomato and sweet onion salad, well dressed with sumac, lemon juice, oil and vinegar.

4 medium potatoes, boiled, peeled and mashed
1 cup fine *burghul*, washed, soaked for 30 minutes, then drained and squeezed
1 large onion
½ cup mint
½ cup parsley
1 teaspoon pimento (allspice)
½ teaspoon cinnamon
1 teaspoon salt
pinch of white pepper
olive oil

Finely chop herbs and onion in a blender and add to potato with spices. Then work *burghul* in, to make a sticky paté. Pack onto a platter, score the surface and drizzle with olive oil.

Kibbe of Potatoes

6 medium potatoes, boiled, peeled and mashed
2 cups fine *burghul*, washed, soaked for 30 minutes, then drained and squeezed
2 large onions, grated
3 teaspoons cinnamon
1 teaspoon salt
1 teaspoon pepper
up to 1 cup plain flour (depending on the stickiness of the potatoes)
oil for baking

Add grated onions and spices to potato and work in *burghul* and flour to make a sticky dough. Place half in a flat, lightly oiled oven dish. Put in either of the fillings and cover with rest of the *kibbe* dough. Score surface, cover with oil and bake at 220°C for about 40 minutes.

Walnut Filling

1 cup walnut pieces
1 cup sultanas

Toast the walnuts for a minute on high in the microwave, careful not to burn. Mix together with sultanas.

Chickpea Filling

1 cup chickpeas
1 cup dried apricots, chopped

Soak chickpeas overnight, drain, then break them in half, by roughly rubbing and squeezing them. Mix with dried apricots.

Onion Filling

1 large onion, sliced in wings
3 tablespoons oil
1 cup walnut pieces
1 cup sultanas
1 teaspoon lemon zest
1 tablespoon lemon juice

Fry onions in oil and add walnuts. Stir on heat briefly, remove then add sultanas, zest and lemon. Stir and reserve.

Kibbe of Potatoes with Herbs

- 6 medium potatoes, boiled, peeled and mashed
- 2 cups fine *burghul*, washed, soaked for 30 minutes, then drained and squeezed
- up to 1 cup plain flour (depending on the stickiness of the potatoes)
- 2 large onions
- 2 cups parsley, loosely packed
- 1 cup mint, loosely packed
- 3 teaspoons pimento (allspice)
- 1 teaspoon cinnamon
- 1 teaspoon salt
- 1 teaspoon pepper
- 100 mL olive oil

Finely chop parsley, mint and onions in processor and add to mashed potato with spices. Add *burghul* and then as much flour as is necessary to make a sticky dough. Press half into a lightly oiled shallow oven dish. Spread with Pine Nut Filling, cover with remaining mixture, score surface, oil top and bake at 200°C for 40–50 minutes, until browned.

Pine Nut Filling

- 3 large onions, sliced in wings
- 2 tablespoons olive oil
- 4 tablespoons pine nuts
- ½ teaspoon salt
- pepper

Fry onions in oil until glazed. Add nuts and seasoning.

Kibbe of Pumpkin

4 cups mashed pumpkin
1½ cups fine *burghul*, washed, soaked for 30 minutes, then drained and squeezed
1 large onion
bunch of leaf coriander
1 orange rind, grated
1 teaspoon salt
1 teaspoon cumin
1 teaspoon pimento (allspice)
½ teaspoon cinnamon
up to 1½ cups plain flour (or plain and besan flour mixed)
pinch of pepper
olive oil

Process onion, coriander, orange rind and spices until fine and add to pumpkin with *burghul* and enough flour to make a sticky dough. Pack half into a lightly oiled, shallow casserole dish. Add filling, cover with the remaining mixture. Score surface and cover with olive oil. Bake at 220°C for 40–50 minutes, until set.

Cumin-flavoured Filling

4 large onions, sliced in wings
3 tablespoons olive oil
1 level teaspoon salt
generous shake of white pepper
3 teaspoons cumin powder
4 tablespoons pine nuts (or 1 cup walnut pieces)

Fry onions in oil until glazed. Add spices and nuts and fry a little longer.

Kibbe of Red Lentils

This recipe comes in part from Paula Wolfert's travels in Gaziantep, Turkey. It keeps well for two days in the fridge. Serve with sweet onions sliced and tossed with sumac, salt and pepper, olive oil and wine vinegar.

1 cup red lentils, boiled in 3 cups salted water until soft and mushy
2 teaspoons tomato paste
2 cloves garlic, crushed
½ cup of coriander leaves, chopped
1 teaspoon ground fenugreek
1 teaspoon ground coriander
pinch of salt
pinch of sugar
1 teaspoon balsamic vinegar
1 teaspoon sweet paprika
1 teaspoon hot chilli, minced
½ cup fine *burghul*, rinsed
1 large onion, finely chopped
2 tablespoons olive oil
pinch of black pepper
1 teaspoon ground cumin
1 tablespoon lemon juice
½ cup chopped parsley
cos lettuce, to serve

Add tomato paste to lentils and stir through. Combine garlic, coriander leaves, fenugreek, ground coriander, salt, sugar, vinegar, paprika and hot chilli and process in a blender until smooth. Add to the saucepan of lentils, stir through and once boiling, remove from the heat. Place *burghul* in a large mixing bowl. Pour hot contents of saucepan over *burghul* and leave to swell for 30 minutes. In a small pan, sauté onion in olive oil, add pepper, cumin and lemon juice. Add the contents of the pan, with parsley, to the lentil mixture and mix. Cool and form into egg-shaped patties. Chill well on a bed of crisp cos lettuce leaves.

KIBBE FOR A MONK (KIBBIT ROHEB)

A vegan dish for an ascetic – animal products are said to arouse the senses. These balls can be added to lentil or Vegetable Soup.

Balls

2 cups fine *burghul*, washed, soaked for 30 minutes, then drained and squeezed
1 cup flour
1 large onion, minced
1 teaspoon salt
1 teaspoon pepper
½ teaspoon chilli

Make a dough with the *burghul*, flour, onion and spices. Knead thoroughly and form into small, marble-size balls.

Soup

1 cup red lentils
250 g spinach, chopped
1 medium onion, chopped
4 cups water
5 cloves garlic
½ teaspoon salt
4 tablespoons olive oil
125 mL lemon juice (or lime juice)

Boil lentils, spinach and onion in water, until tender. Add balls of Kibbe for a Monk and a little more water if necessary and boil for a further 10–15 minutes. Meanwhile, in a food processor, crush the garlic and salt, trickle in the oil and juice, and process further to blend. Add this garlic-lemon sauce to the soup pot to finish.

Kishk, M'jadra, Moughrabieh – comfort food from the heart of this cuisine. *Kishk*, made as it is from fermented yoghurt and wholegrain wheat, is a high protein sustaining food. *M'jadra* is a favourite Friday meal from those meatless Lenten days of yore. *Moughrabieh*, now very fashionable, is a good accompaniment for any protein dish. Vermicelli with Rice is a sure sign that a Lebanese cook is at hand.

All of these are real winter warmers.

Kishk Porridge

Kishk *powder can be bought at many Lebanese grocers.*

1 large onion, finely chopped
2 tablespoons olive oil
1 cup *kishk* powder
1 tomato, chopped, to serve
rice, to serve (or toast)

Fry onion in oil, sprinkle with *kishk* powder and slowly pour on water, stirring to make a smooth paste. Simmer, stirring occasionally, and serve with a little chopped tomato and rice or toast.

Vermicelli with Rice

Sprinkle this with sumac or cinnamon.

2 tablespoons olive oil
1 handful of fine vermicelli, broken
1 cup basmati rice (or other long-grain rice)
1 teaspoon salt
1½ cups water
pinch of sumac, to serve (or cinnamon)

Heat oil and fry vermicelli until it begins to brown. Add rice and salt and stir about. Add water and cook by absorption on a very low heat, or in a rice cooker. Fluff and sprinkle lightly with cinnamon or sumac.

LENTIL AND RICE PATÉ (M'JADRA)

Serve with a tomato-cucumber salad or a crisp cabbage salad.

2 cups brown lentils, soaked overnight and boiled until tender in 4 cups water
¾ cup raw rice
2 large onions, chopped
3 tablespoon oil
pinch of salt

Fry onions in oil until golden. Add to lentils with salt and rice. Simmer, stirring occasionally, until the consistency is like porridge. Pour into a shallow platter and serve at room temperature.

LEBANESE COUSCOUS (MOUGHRABIEH)

These large beads look like large fish roe and swell slightly when cooked.

3 cups water
½ teaspoon salt
olive oil
1 cup Lebanese couscous beads

Bring salted water to the boil with a few drops of olive oil. Pour in couscous beads and boil for 5 minutes. Rinse and add to soups, sauces or vegetable bakes, and continue cooking until tender. Or boil for about 10 minutes, as with pasta, and include as a salad ingredient.

LEBANESE COUSCOUS SALAD

1 cup Lebanese Couscous
1 cup diced beetroot
1 tablespoon black olives, pitted
2 tablespoons feta cheese, crumbled
1 tablespoon pine nuts, toasted
black pepper
2 tablespoons olive oil
1 tablespoon lemon juice
1 tablespoon white wine vinegar

If using raw pine nuts, put them into a small dish and microwave on high for 1 minute to bring out the flavour. Toss all the ingredients well and serve.

There is enough in the world for everybody's need, but not for anybody's greed.

– Mahatma Gandhi

Hands that Cook from a Heart that Hears

'What's the matter, Granny?' I asked her as she shuffled through to the scullery.

'Don't worry,' she said to me, lifting the lid off the fowl food bucket.

'Don't you like it?' I asked her as she scraped Auntie Moine's capsicum and noodle dish off her plate. My aunt dared to try other flavours, to the disdain of her mother-in-law, my Granny Isabel.

That great chronicler of Middle Eastern food and culture, Claudia Roden, once described the Lebanese family as warm and welcoming, but also suffocating. Indeed, one of the greatest strengths is the extended family supporting one another, sharing resources and pain, equally. But sometimes in gatherings of large families such as mine, it looked, and certainly sounded as though no one was listening. Adept simultaneous talkers and eaters, the joke was that we could all eat and talk at once, but no one was seen to speak with a full mouth. Groaning tables were soon laid bare; all replete, some went off to have a nap and others sat quietly in twos or threes, cracking salted pumpkin seeds between their teeth.

Lebanese migrants carry family and foods wherever they go. On the whole, our life in South Africa was materially blessed and the possibilities of such success drew many Lebanese to the place until their immigration was made difficult by the apartheid regime.

Moine's father was one of thousands who fled the Ottoman famine in Lebanon during the First World War. After trying America, he went to South Africa and married his brother's widow, who lived in the town of Cradock on the edge of the Great Karroo in South Africa, where Moine was born in 1925.

After a convent schooling, Moine married Mickey, my mother's brother, just back, with many men of my extended family, from the Second World War. Moine's eyesight had been worrisome for years. Eventually an opthalmologist in East London diagnosed keratoconus (or conical corneas) and told her she would be blind in less than a year. Fortunately she found a doctor who gave her scleral (or haptic) lenses, which cover all parts of the eye.

Moine and Mickey had three children, including Jennifer, my age-mate. I spent a lot of time in their home. In the sitting room, Auntie sat with her embroidery right up to her nose as she covered plain cloths with colourful flowers. After she'd cooked lunch and called us to the table, we obeyed immediately, following the delicious aromas of stuffed vine leaves, white bean stew, or okra ragout. Then she had a rest while we entertained ourselves. After a while, she got up and we followed her to the bathroom where she pulled each eyelid back and inserted the hard glass haptic lens. As she couldn't wear the lens for any length of time, but needed them in order to drive, she had to remove or insert them every few hours, no matter where she was. Sometimes there were six or seven of us children watching her, mouths agape at the sight.

In 1970, Moine became one of the first ten people in South Africa to have a corneal graft. There was no eye bank in those days, so they had to fly to Johannesburg from East London as soon as they got the call. She went on to have four more transplants over the years, managing to keep her sight as her eyes relentlessly changed. Before the transplants, she could not see much with her eyes but as the Xhosa people in South Africa might say, she listened and heard with her heart.

Moine and Mickey were so much a part of my life as I was growing up. They ran a bridge school, teaching scores of East Londoners, including my mother. Whenever there was a family gathering, Moine was there with her laughter and Mickey with a handkerchief: if a single tear fell anywhere in the room, his eyes overflowed at once. Their garden was one where Granny Isabel and I wandered in search of choice pickings.

Moine and Mickey Haddad, 26 December, 1953.

Moine became the one person in our family with whom I could discuss cooking – not just the orthodox recipes of my pedantic grandmother, but flavours from cuisines that Granny ignored, such as those of my Maltese uncle or a Greek cousin. Having grown up in the Karroo beside Afrikaans people, Moine was used to their food and licked her lips when she described creamy Milk Tarts and sugary, fried Koeksusters. Later, when I, as a young housewife, became a vegetarian, Moine collected recipes from magazines and newspapers for me. She was a garlic user – not secretly as my mother's prejudice ordained, but lightly. With pleasure and joy she broadened our knowledge, adding new tastes from the world beyond to our noisy Lebanese feasts.

Kitchen Saints and Their Recipes

I grew up in a privileged home in the old South Africa, where my mother employed a large staff of men and women to run the place. Those women gave up their own families through economic necessity, to come and work in our home. It was impressed on us from early on that the people who worked in our house and garden were in that position because institutionalised racism kept them educationally deprived.

Some of these recipes come from those women whose hard work enriched our lives beyond measure: my Xhosa nursemaid, Rosie Khuselo, whose husband Tata Willie brought Wilson's toffees home after work to all his children, myself included; Katrina Fortuin, our cook, who cursed me, when I was just five years old, for poking my nose into her pots; Katie Harris who broke my mother's ban on garlic and, with ginger and chillies, made the best Saturday omelettes; Dodo or Asma Williams, whose *gesmoorde Kaapse disse* (Cape-style braised dishes) brought out the glutton in us. Louisa Abdurahman abstained during Ramadan while all around her continued eating and drinking; she spoke the King's English in BBC tones and this irritated my mother; perhaps it was the contrast between our flat Eastern Cape vowels and Louisa's rounded-mouth pronunciation. The power struggle between the two women grew until Louisa went back to Cape Town, 'to my own people; they are of a higher class than you here in East London'.

The special dishes and style of these cooks gave me a template from which many of my own recipes in this chapter are drawn.

Rosie was my nursemaid from the time I was born until I turned five and went to school. She used to take me far down the garden, near the compost pits where puff adders hid, to gather wild spinach (*m'finu*). One evening, impatient for my supper, I pulled the boiling pot of *m'finu* off the kitchen bench. Fortunately, I was not hurt, unlike the morning when I was two years old and tried to jump from my high chair to grab at the *maltabella* (malted sorghum) porridge she was cooling at the window. My teeth went through my lower lip, and my father was called from his office to drive me to the surgery.

In Australia the community of ex-South Africans is as diverse as the country itself. Some are born and bred Africans, while others, until they left, were guests or travellers in South Africa for one or two generations. What we have in common is that we were born into and lived a formative part of our years in a bedevilled place. Food memories take us to the African mothers who loved and fed us on many levels. Despite their pain and the difficulties of their lives, as kitchen saints they had it in their hearts to nurture us while their children were mostly much worse off.

At school, I had long conversations with Sister Johanna, my kindergarten teacher. As a young Swiss woman, she'd left home to be a missionary in Africa. I had the privilege of being close to her over many years, at times discussing the pain of life for all in apartheid South Africa. When I was fourteen, she gave me this prayer, a recipe for my life.

Leaven

A little bit is sufficient to make an entire loaf rise. Without leaven, the dough remains sluggish, sunken in itself. If one throws leaven into the kneading trough, it disappears but still works on. I have received all my talents that they may be a leaven in the world. Thrown into the mass of my environment, my life seems to be without meaning. I often doubt myself, and my power to radiate goodness; but with grace, the dough of humanity will slowly rise without my noticing it. Do not let me be satisfied with a mediocre life. Let me find the leaven in my most inner being and filled with grace, let me be the leaven of my environment.

Cecile, in kindergarten, age seven, second row from bottom, last on the right with Sister Magdelenis, 1960.

Rosie's Cornmeal with Spinach and Sour Milk

(Mieliemeel, M'finu and Amasi)

Amasi *is soured milk and* mieliemeel *is finely ground cornmeal, for which you can use instant polenta*

1 medium onion, sliced
1 tablespoon oil
small bunch of spinach, chopped
(or dandelion greens)
125 g cornmeal (or instant polenta)
pinch of salt
shake of white pepper
amasi, to serve

Fry onion in oil. Add spinach and cook until wilted. Sprinkle cornmeal onto spinach and allow to cook for a further 10 minutes on low heat. Serve with *amasi.*

Katrina's Cracked Corn Samp and Beans (Ngqush)

In my childhood home, Saturday was known as ngqush *(*samp *and beans) day; we ate it with farm sausage (*boerewors*) and perhaps some eggplant in oil (*buttenjen ata*) left over from Friday's Catholic meat-free meals. Katrina was our cook for many years. A rotund personality, she had a great laugh on her until alcohol ate into her life and she had to retire.*

2 cups *samp* (cracked corn)
1 cup kidney beans

Rinse and soak together overnight in plenty of water. Rinse, cover with fresh water and boil until tender. Season and serve as a vegetable.

Corn and Bean Soup Katrina's Ngqush soup

3 cups brown beans, soaked overnight
3 cups corn kernels, cooked
2 teaspoons salt
pepper

Rinse beans and boil until tender. Add corn and seasoning and boil for about 30 minutes, until soupy. A dash of butter may be added to each serving.

Crumbly Cornmeal (Pokkoquo in Xhosa, Krummelpap in Afrikaans)

This recipe uses mieliemeel *(fine cornmeal) or instant polenta.*

½ cup water
½ teaspoon salt
1 cup fine cornmeal (or instant polenta)
amasi, to serve (or gravy)

Boil water and salt and pour cornmeal into a pyramid in the centre of the pot. Cover and steam on low for about 15 minutes. Break up with a fork into crumbly bits and allow to simmer for 20 more minutes until soft. Serve with *amasi* or gravy.

Corn Pudding (Mieliepoeding)

A soft corn cake.

4 cups corn kernels
2 tablespoons honey
1 egg
½ cup milk
1 level teaspoon baking powder
1 tablespoon flour (wheat, corn or rice)

Mix all ingredients in a food processor until a chunky batter results. Pour into an oiled 1-litre pudding bowl and cover. Microwave on medium for 15 minutes, until firm. May also be covered with foil in which a few holes have been pierced and steamed for 60 minutes.

Farm-style Beans and Potatoes (Boereboontjies)

250 g French cut green beans
250 g peeled, diced potatoes
1 small onion, finely chopped
water to just cover
salt
white pepper

Boil the ingredients until almost no liquid remains. Mash together and season with salt and pepper.

Cabbage Braised with Pumpkin (Gesmoorde Kool met Pampoen)

250 g white cabbage, cut in large slices
400 g pumpkin, thinly sliced
2 tablespoons oil
2 medium onions, sliced
1 clove garlic, crushed
1 tablespoon grated ginger
1 mild green chilli, chopped
3 peeled tomatoes, cut in chunks
pinch of salt
white pepper

Heat oil and fry onions. Add garlic, ginger and chilli, then cabbage and pumpkin. Cover and allow to cook in the juices for about 20 minutes. Add tomatoes and continue simmering until everything is tender. Season and serve hot.

Louisa's Stewed Water Hyacinth (Waterblommetjie Bredie)

2 cups water hyacinth
1 tablespoon oil
1 x 5 cm cassia stick
1 medium onion, diced
3 medium potatoes, sliced
pinch of salt
white pepper
handful of chopped sorrel
  (or 2 tablespoons lemon juice)
1 cup vegetable stock
rice, to serve

If the flowers are fresh, rinse repeatedly to remove grit and soak for a few hours in salt water to clean. Heat oil with cassia stick and sauté onion. Add potatoes, seasoning, sorrel and flowers. Pour over stock and simmer on low until all tender. Serve with rice.

TOMATO STEW THERESA'S TAMATIE BREDIE

Theresa was a wonderful woman who came to work for us when I was thirteen. We became close friends until she died, tragically young, from breast cancer.

3 tablespoons oil
2 x 5 cm cassia sticks
8 cloves
2 large onions, sliced
2 cloves garlic
1 tablespoon grated ginger
1 teaspoon minced chilli
salt
1 star anise
1 heaped teaspoon ground cumin
1 teaspoon ground coriander
600 mL crushed tomatoes
3 tablespoons tomato paste
200 g green beans, whole
1 medium eggplant, diced
2 zucchini, cut in chunks
2 cups carrot, sliced thickly
rice, to serve

Heat oil and fry cassia and cloves until they begin to change colour. Add onions and stir about. Then add garlic, ginger, chilli and the rest of the spices. Stir well over heat for a few minutes. Then add tomatoes and the remaining vegetables. Stir well. Simmer, adding a tiny bit of water if necessary, until all tender. Serve with rice.

RICE WITH PEAS (BIRYANI) FOR A MALAY FEAST

If you'd like to have a real Cape feast, here is Dodo's biryani, *which can be served with a variety of side dishes. It is especially good served with cabbage braise, Tomato Stew, Eggplant Braise and Cucumber Cooler.*

- 2 cups basmati rice, cooked and set aside
- 1 cup brown or green lentils, cooked and set aside
- 2 large onions, diced
- 1 star anise
- 12 curry leaves
- 3 cardamom pods
- 8 cloves
- 1 small bay leaf
- 1 x 3 cm cassia stick
- 1 tablespoon fennel seeds
- 500 g shelled peas (or mixed vegetables)
- 1 teaspoon turmeric
- 2 teaspoons ground cumin
- 2 teaspoons coriander

Fry onions in a little oil, add whole spices and stir well. Add the rest of the ingredients and a dash of water and simmer until peas are tender. In a deep dish, layer half the lentils, then half the rice, all of the pea (or vegetable) mixture, the rest of the rice and finish with lentils. Dot with butter, then cover and bake at 180°C for about 35 minutes, or heat in the microwave for 15–20 minutes on medium to high.

DODO'S DATE AND TAMARIND RELISH

Dodo (or Dorothy) was a wonderful Malay grandmother who babysat my son until she retired when he was five years old. She taught me her mother's cooking secrets – simple food prepared with an abundance of love. When she converted to Islam, she changed her name to Asma.

- 1 cup dates, stoned
- 1 tablespoon tamarind purée
- 1 large onion
- 8 cloves garlic
- 4 small hot red chillies, seeded
- ½ cup cider vinegar
- large handful of fresh coriander

Blend all ingredients in a food processor until a chunky paste results. Store in jars in refrigerator and serve with curries or rice dishes.

Katie's Slow-baked Lentil Curry
(Gesmoorde Lensieskerrie)

2 tablespoons oil
2 large onions, sliced
1 capsicum, sliced
2 cloves garlic
2 teaspoons fragrant curry powder
2 teaspoons cumin
1 teaspoon turmeric
1 star anise
1 cup brown or green lentils, washed
1 bay leaf
large handful of parsley, chopped
4 tablespoons tomato purée
3 cups water
½ teaspoon salt
½ teaspoon pepper

Sauté onions, capsicum and garlic in oil. Add spices and fry gently. Add the remaining ingredients, except salt, with 3 cups water and bake, covered, at 180°C for about 45 minutes, until soft. Add salt, stir through and cook for 5 more minutes.

Lentil Curry Pies (Pasteie)

Serve with chutney or Dodo's Date and Tamarind Relish.

Katie's Slow-baked Lentil Curry

Allow Katie's Slow-baked Lentil Curry to cool, drop spoonfuls in puff pastry squares, pinch into squares or pasty shapes and bake at 200°C for about 15 minutes, until browned. Serve with chutney or Dodo's Date and Tamarind Relish.

Katie's Saturday Omelette with Garlic

Katie Harris was a strong character who brooked no opposition in her kitchen. By the time she came to work for us, my mother was quite happy to hand over all of the cooking to Katie. She and I were great friends and she initiated me into the delights of a sensuous life, with great humour and mischief.

1 medium onion, finely chopped
2 tablespoons oil
3 medium tomatoes, chopped
1 teaspoon grated fresh ginger
3 cloves garlic, crushed
1 medium to hot red chilli
1 level teaspoon turmeric
½ teaspoon hot curry powder (masala)
salt
shake of pepper
8 eggs
small bunch of coriander, lightly chopped

Sauté onions in oil, add the rest of the ingredients (except eggs and coriander) and simmer until softened. Beat eggs lightly and pour over, stirring a little at first, and then leave to set. Garnish with chopped coriander to serve.

Parsnip and Apple Curry

500 g parsnips, peeled sliced and boiled until just tender
2 tablespoons oil
8 cloves
3 bay leaves
3 large onions, sliced in rings
2 teaspoons mild fragrant curry powder
375 mL water from parsnips with ½ vegetable stock cube
1 cup cooked apple pieces, still whole
2 teaspoons flour
80 mL cider vinegar
rice, to serve

Heat oil and temper with cloves and bay leaves. Add onions and stir about until they begin to colour. Add curry powder, fry briefly and add parsnips, stock and apples. Mix flour with vinegar and add all to boiling saucepan. Allow to thicken and serve hot with rice, or cold as a side dish.

Asma's Spicy Pea Soup (Groenertjie Sop)

This is the Malay version.

2 cups green split peas
1 bay leaf
8 whole cloves
8 pimento (allspice) berries
10 black peppercorns
1 x 3 cm cassia stick
2 large carrots, scraped
1 large onion
1 large potato
1 medium turnip (or swede)
1 medium parsnip
2 medium, red tomatoes
3 celery sticks, with leaves
handful of parsley
smaller handful of mint
2 cloves garlic
salt

Put peas into a large pot and cover with cold water. Add all the spices (bay leaves, cloves, pimento berries, peppercorns and cassia stick tied in a small square of muslin) and boil until tender. Add the rest of the ingredients and boil until soft. Remove spice bag, press between two spoons to release flavours into the saucepan, and discard. Purée the soup until smooth and add salt to taste.

Curried Bananas

2 medium onions, diced
2 tablespoons oil
3 cloves
2 cardamon pods
6 curry leaves
1 teaspoon turmeric
1 teaspoon fennel seeds
1 teaspoon ground cumin
pinch of cayenne
3 tomatoes, diced
3 large bananas, quartered
1 tablespoon coriander leaves, chopped
hard-boiled eggs, peeled and halved (optional)

Sauté onions in oil. Add spices and stir about. Add tomatoes and, when reduced, add bananas and finish off with coriander. Peeled, halved hard-boiled eggs may be added, yolk down, at the last minute.

Pumpkin Curry with Peas

A fragrant shortcut.

2 large onions, quartered
8 cloves garlic
1 tin (410 g) tomatoes
1 fresh, medium to hot red chilli
1 tablespoon ginger, grated
4 tablespoons oil
6 whole cloves
1 stick lemongrass, white part bruised, green part made into 125 mL tea
1 teaspoon turmeric
1 teaspoon fenugreek
1½ cups frozen peas
5 cups golden pumpkin, cut into chunks (or butternut)
1 cup coriander, coarsely chopped
1 level teaspoon salt

Put the onions, garlic, tomatoes, chilli and ginger into a food processor and blend until chunky. Heat oil and cloves in pot. Add processed tomato mixture to pot and fry for about 7 minutes, stirring from time to time. Add lemongrass, turmeric, fenugreek, peas and pumpkin with the lemongrass tea. Stir every few minutes, simmering until everything is tender. Test for salt – should take about 1 level teaspoon. Finish with coriander.

Curried Vegetable Bake

A combination of sweet vegetables: assemble in a matter of minutes. Long melon is a green vegetable found in most Lebanese and Chinese greengrocers.

1 medium onion, diced
1 large carrot, sliced
2 cups long melon, peeled and diced
less than 1 cup red lentils, rinsed
1 tablespoon oil
1 tablespoon tomato paste
1½ cups boiling water
1 x 5 cm cassia stick
1 bay leaf
1 small star anise
1 teaspoon mild curry powder
1 heaped teaspoon ground coriander
½ teaspoon turmeric
3 tablespoons plain yoghurt, to finish
bread, to serve (or rice)

Toss all ingredients, except yoghurt, together in a casserole dish. Cover and bake at 190°C for an hour. Stir yoghurt through, return to oven for 7 minutes and serve with bread or rice.

QUINCE AND POTATO CURRY (GESMOORDE KWEPER)

Quinces grew well in the Karroo, and farmers' wives made sweet pastes and jellies. This curry can be served on rice with yoghurt and cucumber.

2 tablespoons oil
3 medium quinces, peeled, cored and cubed
2 bay leaves
6 cloves
1 teaspoon cumin seeds
½ teaspoon fennel seeds
2 cloves garlic, crushed
1 large onion, chopped
4 medium potatoes, peeled and cubed
1 teaspoon paprika
1 teaspoon turmeric
½ teaspoon chilli powder
2 teaspoons ground coriander
1 level teaspoon fenugreek
little water
½ teaspoon salt
pepper

Heat oil and seal quince pieces briefly, remove and set aside. Add whole spices to oil and allow to just change colour then sauté garlic and onion. Add potatoes and other spices and stir about. Add very little water and bring to a simmer for 5 minutes. Then add quince pieces and simmer until everything is tender. There should be a little thick sauce around the vegetables.

The act of putting into your mouth what the earth has grown is perhaps your most direct interaction with the earth.

– Frances Moore Lappé,
Diet for a Small Planet

Hunting and Gathering: Finding a Wondercushion!

'It's very nice,' my mother said, looking into her plate. She faced me across the table, 'Did you put garlic in here?'

I sort of smiled thinking to myself, *Here we go again, my mother and her pet hate.*

'*Sies*!' she said, and pursed her lips. Turning to my father, she said, 'This one uses anything and everything in her cooking. Next thing it'll be weeds from the garden.'

As a cook, I trawl the four directions for unusual ingredients. It is on these searches that I have discovered the hidden and undisclosed parts of people and places. My first foray, as a teenage cook in South Africa, was into East London's Indian bazaar, where Mrs Patel asked me, 'What you cooking, dear?'

'Please can you tell me what to do with these lentils?' I asked, and she filled my arms with dahls, ginger, chillis, garlic, and incense. At home under the cover of a cloud of jasmine that rose up on the kitchen windowsill, I added the peeled and crushed garlic to my saucepan. My mother wouldn't know about it until her first mouthful.

On a visit home from university in Grahamstown, during a terrible drought, Auntie Moine directed me to a little shop in town where I could stock up on dehydrated vegetables. At the door, a plaque in Zulu said '*Kupugani*': 'Uplift yourself', in English. The organisation was started in the late 1960s, by Barbara Follett, the British Labour MP, and her then husband Rick Turner, a South African political philosopher, as a response to starvation.

That afternoon in 1972, a well-coiffed matron showed me the high-protein biscuits and soup for starving African children who managed to get to school or a clinic. On a shelf behind her, small brown packets of different kinds of beans, corn in many forms and an array of dehydrated vegetables were packed together. As I mulled over the products, the place began to fill with African workers who came shopping at lunchtime.

I left there with dehydrated onions and extruded tomato paste that looked like red All Bran, dried soya bits and powdered milk. At the supermarket down the road, porters pushed overloaded trolleys for affluent shoppers, while housewives left the Kupugani shop with a packet of beans and *mieliemeel* porridge to feed nine or ten. Despite harrowing political times, during which Rick Turner was assassinated in front of his children and Barbara fled to Britain, the Kupugani organisation still feeds generations all over that country.

Meanwhile, as the drought around Grahamstown worsened, the farmers' wives began a cooperative called Home Industries. We, university students living in local digs, purchased cakes, biscuits, handicrafts and, above all, the freshest produce from their farm gardens sustained with bathroom and laundry grey water. There were bunches of silverbeet, parsley, spring onions and eggplants; in winter, chestnuts and enormous cabbages. Many farms were saved from ruin by this enterprise.

When I moved to Cape Town, my vegetarian friend Lisha suggested I try Compassion, a hunger-relief organisation, for beans. In a rundown building near the children's hospital, a plump woman stood behind a counter with blonde hair and a fag hanging from her moving lips.

'Hello, howzit?' she said.

I hesitated and then asked her, 'What do you do here?'

'*Ach* man, these poor people here will use their last cent if they have to boil these soya beans for hours and hours. So some church people from England came and taught us about these insulating cushions for cooking.'

She hauled out a poylstyrene-filled bag made by women in the nearby squatter camp. I hung around and watched her advising a group from a local township, accepting donations and sending a man in an old pickup to drop fabric at a sewing group on the Cape Flats. For me, the rest is history. I was hooked, and visited her from time to time to learn, and to dig myself deeper into the hidden layers of a society of such wealth and such poverty within a mile of each other, and me.

The Bo-Kaap, Malay quarter, Upper Wale Street, Cape Town.

Looking for spices, I set off on a bright spring morning for the Bo-kaap in Upper Wale Street, with its view across the city to Table Bay Harbour. The steep streets are lined with nineteenth-century cottages built by descendants of

Malay and Javanese slaves, brought by ships of the Dutch East India Company to build the new settlement of Cape Town. Tilers and stonemasons applied their skills to these houses and mosques – the character of the place is unmistakable.

My twitching nose registered my destination: Atlas Trading, the best spice merchants anywhere. Sacks of lentils, rice and dried chillis stood beside the doorway. A Malay man with a flat, round *kufea* on his head sat behind a glassed-in booth: no one left the shop before paying respects to the cashier and his adding machine. Women wearing colourful beaded veiling *medoras* on their heads and men in various skullcaps carried large-scale purchases out to their cars. During Ramadan, the staff worked hardest on empty stomachs to supply the makings of fast-breaking meals to crowds of customers. Apartheid horrors could have been forgotten in such a place, except the *kramat* on nearby Signal Hill, one of a number of shrines to Muslim saints, who were brought to the place as slaves and died there, is a reminder of the Imam Haron, murdered by the security police in 1969, just five years before I was there.

On the way home, I stopped at Salt River market for okra, eggplants and green coriander. The *waterblommetjie* (water hyacinth) vendor at the market was famous for her angry retort to a journalist who queried the freshness of her product.

'*Yessus, merrem*!' she had shouted. 'I been up to my tits in cold water at four o'clock this morning to get this for you and you ask me if it's fresh!'

As it was a Tuesday, I went home via a grocery store run by a Chinese family. I took my container to the back of the shop where the grandmother filled it with tofu that she made every Monday night.

Cooking in South Africa took me out and about, discovering life in the land of my birth. But what of my mother's garlic phobia? It was only in old age that she told me how as a girl of twelve at the convent in Queenstown, she was standing in line one day with her classmates when one of them turned around to her and said, loudly, '*Sies*, you stink. What have you been eating?'

She and her older sister Phyllis went home and told their mother they would refuse to eat any food at all, until she could show that all garlic in the house had been thrown out. Mercifully, I live in a different time, in another world, where shame is mostly about what we do and no longer about who we are.

Proteins from Plants

Welcome to the wonderful world of pulses and legumes, a place that daunts some, bringing to mind questions like 'how do I cook them?' and terrifying us with the threat of nuclear gas eruptions, and therefore questions like 'how do I avoid them?' and 'why bother with this risky food?'

Beans are a valuable source of protein for vegetarians. They also contain a good selection of minerals, such as potassium, iron, calcium, magnesium and zinc, and vitamins, especially those in the B group.

You may wonder about a whole section on tofu, when some hate it, some use it daily, some have to eat it regularly and some are told to avoid it.

In the 1960s, when the West discovered soya beans, a staple in Asia for millennia, we all thought we were going to live forever! As we age, however, many of us have decided we'd rather live the present moment in as good a shape as possible. Tofu adds great variety and nutrition – high-quality protein and calcium – to a vegetarian or vegan diet.

There are different kinds of tofu: these recipes are for plain, unsmoked, unfermented tofu. Silken tofu is good for dips and desserts (instead of cream). Silken firm tofu is great for scrambling. Firm tofu is recommended in most of these recipes.

To make textured tofu, freeze a block of firm tofu for about thirty-six hours, thaw thoroughly, squeeze out all the water and pull the tofu apart, or cut it into the required shape for cooking. It will have a slightly chewy texture and absorb sauces and flavours very well. An important note: tofu, once opened, should be stored in a dish of cold water in the fridge for no more than twenty-four hours. I have the same time limit for cooked tofu.

Legumes, pulses and tofu enrich any diet. The fat-saving and fibre-enhancing qualities are excellent when used as a substitute for a meat meal, and the low glycaemic index of these recipes is helpful to people with fluctuating blood-sugar levels.

Tips for Legumes and Pulses

Cooking

To reduce flatulence from eating legumes, they should be soaked overnight and thoroughly rinsed before cooking in enough water to cover them well.

If you're in a hurry and have forgotten to pre-soak, put the required quantity in a saucepan, cover with boiling water, bring to the boil and cook for five minutes. Remove from the heat, then cover and set aside for one hour. Rinse thoroughly, cover with fresh water and cook until tender.

To make very soft chickpeas for *fatteh* or Chickpeas with Tahini, my friend Loubna suggests the following: rinse the chickpeas you've soaked overnight, cover with fresh water, stir in half a teaspoon of bi-carb and allow to stand for 10 minutes. Then wash the chickpeas a couple of times to get rid of the bi-carb, cover with fresh water and boil. You will need to keep skimming the surface foam until it clears.

You may use beans in a casserole or stew directly after soaking, but this will then require long, slow cooking. Cooking times vary:

soya beans	up to 2 hours, after soaking
chickpeas	about 40 minutes, after soaking
flat white lima beans (or butter beans)	30–50 minutes, after soaking
kidney beans/canellini/borlotti beans	45–60 minutes, after soaking
brown and green lentils, mung beans and black eye peas	20–40 minutes, after soaking
split red lentils and green split peas	15 and 40 minutes, respectively

Split red lentils lack the cellulose skin of the other pulses, so soaking is therefore not necessary. Simply rinse well before use. Also remember the older the legume, the longer it will take to cook, and that different recipes call for legumes cooked to different stages: barely cooked, still firm (al dente), almost cooked, well-cooked, or even mushy (as with chickpeas for making smooth *humous*).

To ensure that legumes cook through and soften, salt is only added in the last five minutes of the boiling process, never before they are at the desired stage of tenderness or they will remain hard.

If you've cooked too many legumes for that stew or soup, allow them to cool and seal the remainder in a plastic container in the fridge for up to three days. Also remember that cooked beans freeze very well.

Decorum

Wilfred Thesiger's chronicles of his 1940s travels in the Near East reveal what has now been lost to tyranny: his classic descriptions of life in the Empty Quarter and among the Marsh Arabs of Iraq are testament to his literary genius in taking the reader right back into that time and place.

He told an apocryphal story that illustrates the complete unacceptability of farting in Arab culture – where burping, on the other hand, is applause for the cook. In the story, a young man accidentally let one go while attending the meeting house with the elders for the first time. No one said a word. He knew what he had to do: he simply got up and started walking. For years he walked until he reached Upper Egypt, where he lived among the Nubians.

As an old man, he set off once more, walking through seasons to reach his home village. On the outskirts he met a young man.

'When were you born?' the old man asked.

'I was born in the year of the fart outside the meeting house.'

This reply sent the shamed man walking all the way back to Nubia.

When I was writing *Book of Legumes*, I was deluged with fart jokes. Someone in South Africa sent me a cartoon of Auntie Maggie's powerful bean soup that blew the bloomers off Hagar the Horrible.

In Australia the fart is feared only for its possible consequence. Such as when Brian was off to pick up Kylie for a date. He arrived while she was still getting ready and her mother ushered him into the living room, where her father was reading the newspaper. Brian sat on a chair, under which the family dog was snoring. Brian was nervous and his tummy started to rumble. Wind built up and he thought he'd just let one go quietly and they'd think it was the dog. Well, it was a stinker. But he felt fine as old Fido was still snoring under there.

Another suddenly arrived and this one felt very urgent. He discreetly shifted his bottom on the seat, and whew! thank heavens for Fido, he thought.

He sat quietly, wishing Kylie would hurry up, when it felt as though the whole nachos lunch was trying to flee his gut. One last time, he thought, and suddenly Kylie's mother screamed, 'Fido, Fido, come out from under there before he shits on you!'

We all think we can blame the dog but we usually get caught. Although Lucy, my Labrador-Beagle cross, was never a vegetarian, she loved most vegetables and stole food at every opportunity. From her bed in my writing space, she let off digestive aromas until the ripe old age of fifteen.

Following the exhortation to soak and rinse beans before cooking can be face-saving.

Lucy.

Tofu

Afelia with Tofu

A traditional Greek dish with a thick sauce.

500 g textured tofu
4 tablespoons olive oil
2 tablespoons whole coriander seeds
2 large onions, cut in chunks
2 large carrots, cut in chunks
ground black pepper
1 cup red wine
2 cloves garlic, crushed
2 teaspoons tomato paste
1 cup cooked brown beans
rice, steamed, to serve (or crusty bread)

Heat the oil in a large saucepan and fry the coriander seeds until they start to change colour. Then add the onions, carrots and pepper. Stir about. Add wine, garlic, tomato paste and beans with a little of their cooking water. Add shredded tofu and stir through. Bake in a deep, covered casserole dish at 180°C for at least an hour, until cooked through and the sauce has thickened. Serve with steamed rice or crusty bread.

Jericho Tofu

Traditional Palestinian flavours. Great when served with rice and a salad of mint, parsley and tomato with lemon and oil dressing.

200 g textured tofu, shredded
3 tablespoons olive oil
2 x 3 cm cassia sticks
1 large onion, sliced in wings
2 cloves garlic, crushed
2 tablespoon pine nuts
1 teaspoon pimento (allspice)
2 teaspoons sumac
pinch of salt
pinch of black pepper
2 tablespoons lemon juice

Heat oil in a saucepan with cassia sticks. Add onions and stir about until beginning to brown. Add tofu, garlic and pine nuts. Stir well. Add spices and stir-fry. Sprinkle lemon juice over.

Chilli Con Tofu

250 g textured tofu, shredded
2 tablespoons oil
2 onions, chopped
2 cloves garlic, crushed
1 teaspoon paprika
1 teaspoon cumin
2 bay leaves
1 tablespoon coriander powder
pinch of salt
pinch of pepper
½ teaspoon medium to hot chilli powder
250 mL vegetable stock
1 tin (410 g) tomatoes and juice
2 cups cooked red kidney beans
small handful of fresh oregano, roughly snipped
rice, to serve

Sauté onion and garlic in oil. Add tofu and stir about. Add spices and stir through. Add vegetable stock and simmer for 5 minutes. Add tomatoes, beans and oregano and simmer for about 5 minutes. Serve with rice.

Tofu Sour Cream

Delicious with chopped fresh herbs, on baked potatoes.

1 cup silken tofu
3 tablespoons oil
3 tablespoons cider vinegar
1 teaspoon lemon juice
2 teaspoons sugar
salt

Blend all together until smooth. Cover and refrigerate.

TOFU BALLS (KAFTA)

Adapted from a Lebanese favourite.

Tofu

300 g firm tofu
1 medium onion
small bunch of parsley
½ small bunch of mint
1 teaspoon pimento (allspice)
pinch of white pepper
pinch of cinnamon
2 cups soft breadcrumbs
(or 1 cup cooked rice)

Blend all ingredients in food processor, form into balls and place in an oiled casserole dish. Pour sauce over balls and bake at 200°C for 30 minutes.

Sauce

1 tablespoon tomato paste
1 cup vegetable stock
1 cup boiling water
1 x 3 cm cassia stick

Mix together.

TOFU LOAF

Use the same ingredients for Tofu Balls, plus:

6 medium potatoes, boiled, peeled and left aside to cool and dry out, then sliced or grated
olive oil, to paint
Tofu Sour Cream, to serve

Blend all Tofu Balls ingredient well in a food processor, form into a loaf and place in a deep oven dish. Mix sauce ingredients together and pour over the loaf. Place potato over the top. Paint lightly with oil. Bake at 200°C for 30 minutes. Serve with Tofu Sour Cream.

Kebabs of Tofu

Don't feel left out at a bbq – they'll all be wanting yours! Serve on rice with sweet chilli or satay sauce, and a salad.

250 g firm tofu, cut into 5 cm cubes
1 large red onion, cut into cubes
1 green capsicum, cut into squares

Marinade

1 tablespoon oil
1 tablespoon honey
1 tablespoon sherry
1 tablespoon soya sauce
1 teaspoon tomato paste
1 clove garlic, crushed
1 green chilli, sliced

Stir all marinade ingredients together and place tofu cubes in to steep for a few hours. Thread onto skewers with onion and capsicum, then barbecue or oven grill.

Noodles with Tofu and Nuts

1 packet (200 g) Thai rice stick noodles, softened in water as directed
350 g firm tofu, diced
3 tablespoons olive oil
1 large onion, cut lengthwise in 1 cm slices
1 red capsicum, sliced
3 cups bean sprouts
½ bunch of shallots, cut in diagonal slices
1 cup macadamia nut pieces (or cashew pieces)
2 tablespoons chilli sauce
2 tablespoons soya sauce
2 tablespoons fruit chutney

Heat oil and stir-fry onion and capsicum. Add tofu cubes and heat through. Toss remaining ingredients through, add noodles, heat thoroughly and serve.

Lasagne with Tofu

Other vegetables may be added to this dish – for example, lightly steamed and chopped spinach, grilled eggplant slices, roasted capsicum or Grilled Mushrooms.

400 g silken tofu
375 g red lentils, boiled until tender
box (250 g) lasagne sheets
2 tablespoons oil
1 leek, shredded
2 large carrots, shredded
1 medium white turnip, shredded
2 cloves garlic, crushed
ground black pepper
3 cups pulverised tomatoes (or pasta sauce)
1 vegetable stock cube
2 cups water
1 teaspoon oregano, dried
handful of fresh basil leaves, roughly torn
3 medium zucchini in long slices, steamed until just tender

Heat oil in a large pan and sweat leek, carrot and turnip on low heat to wilt. Add the rest of the ingredients, except the tofu, zucchini and lasagne sheets, and boil up for a few minutes. Remove from heat and stir tofu through. Layer sauce with instant lasagne sheets and zucchini slices in a deep dish, ending with sauce. Bake for 45 minutes at 180°C.

Mint and Lemon Tofu Slices

400 g firm tofu, cut into 2-cm-thick slices and covered well with flour
80 mL lemon juice
80 mL olive oil
2 teaspoons mint, dried
salad, to serve

Heat oil in frying pan and fry tofu slices, turning once. Pour on lemon juice and shake pan to thicken sauce. Sprinkle with dried mint and serve with a salad.

Mushroom Tofu Snack

1 tub (375 g) silken tofu
1 medium onion, finely chopped
1 tablespoon olive oil
2 cups brown mushrooms, finely chopped
2 tablespoons pine nuts
(or slivered almonds)
salt
pepper
pinch of cinnamon
pinch of sumac
½ teaspoon pimento (allspice)
pre-cooked pizza base

Sauté onion in oil until soft. Turn up heat and add the rest of the ingredients, except tofu, and stir about until cooked. Allow to cool, then stir tofu through until well mixed. Bake on a pre-cooked pizza base at 180°C for about 15 minutes until slightly browned.

Mustardy Mushrooms with Tofu

Marinade

2 tablespoons olive oil
2 tablespoons soya sauce
1 tablespoon whole grain French mustard
1 tablespoon balsamic vinegar

Mix all ingredients.

Mushrooms

300 g firm tofu, diced
3 cups mushrooms, sliced
1 large onion, sliced
3 tablespoons olive oil
rice and peas, to serve

Pour marinade over onion, mushrooms and tofu and allow to stand, in the fridge, for about 5 hours. Heat the 3 tablespoons olive oil in a wok or large pan and tip the tofu mushroom mixture in. Stir-fry until the mushrooms are tender and serve with cooked rice and peas.

Pastry with Tofu

350 g silken tofu
1 tablespoon salt
3 cups flour
½ cup warm water

Knead ingredients together and roll to make top and bottom crusts or small pies. Bake at 190–200°C for approximately 12 minutes.

Peas with Tofu

300 g firm tofu, cut into 2 cm cubes
250 g green peas
1 large onion, chopped
4 red tomatoes
3 cloves garlic, peeled
2 teaspoons ginger, grated
1 hot green chilli
1 tablespoon fennel seeds
1 teaspoon ground coriander
pinch of salt
1 tablespoon coriander, chopped, for garnish

Add onion, tomatoes, garlic, ginger and chilli to a food processor and blend to a chunky consistency. Fry fennel seeds in hot oil until they start to change colour. Add tomato mixture and stir about. Add peas, salt and ground coriander, cover and simmer for 10 minutes, adding a little water if necessary. Add tofu, allow to heat through, garnish with coriander and serve.

PEPPER TOFU AFTER AJOY JOSHI

350 g firm tofu, squeezed and cut into 2 cm by 5 cm slices
½ teaspoon salt
1 teaspoon black peppercorns, freshly crushed
less than ½ teaspoon of chilli powder (or more, depending on taste)
1 teaspoon ground coriander
1 teaspoon tamarind concentrate in 125 mL hot water
8 fresh curry leaves, torn
2 teaspoons ginger, grated
1 teaspoon crushed garlic
2 tablespoons oil
1 tablespoon coriander, chopped, for garnish

Marinate tofu in all ingredients, except oil, for about 1 hour, in fridge. Heat oil and toss tofu for about 3 minutes. Serve warm, garnished with coriander.

QUICHE WITH TOFU AND HERBS

300 g silken tofu, beaten to a creamy consistency
½ cup chopped shallots
½ cup chopped parsley
ground black pepper
pinch of salt
2 cups boiled potato, grated

Add herbs and shallots to creamed tofu, add seasoning and stir. Place grated boiled potato in an oiled casserole dish, pour tofu mixture over and bake at 180°C, until firm.

Almost Niçoise Salad

This is a version of niçoise salad that contains no egg or tuna.

Marinade

3 tablespoons lemon juice
2 tablespoons olive oil
1 tablespoon chopped chives
1 clove garlic, crushed
2 tablespoons chopped parsley
1 teaspoon dried oregano
½ teaspoon black pepper
pinch of salt

Mix all ingredients.

Tofu

1 cup firm tofu, cubed

Lay tofu in the marinade and allow to stand in the fridge for a few hours.

Salad

2 medium tomatoes, quartered
handful of salad leaves
1 Lebanese cucumber, peeled and sliced
1 cup green beans, steamed
2 tablespoons black olives

Toss ingredients together, add marinated tofu and serve.

Tofu Salad with Cabbage and Cashews

Salad

300 g firm tofu, sliced into
 3 x 10 cm fingers
olive oil
3 cups finely sliced red cabbage
3 or 4 tablespoons soya sauce
1 cup carrot, sliced into matchsticks
1 medium red onion, thinly sliced
1 cup toasted cashew nuts
sweet chilli sauce

Pat the tofu dry and dip into the soya sauce. Drizzle very lightly with olive oil and grill until the tofu is just beginning to brown. In a large bowl, spread cabbage, carrot and onion. Top with warm tofu, sprinkle with dressing, scatter nuts and add a small dollop of chilli sauce.

Dressing

1 teaspoon minced garlic
1 tablespoon chopped mint
1 tablespoon grated ginger
1 teaspoon lime zest
3 tablespoons lime juice
Thai basil, to garnish

Mix all ingredients, except basil, and pour over salad. Garnish with basil.

SPICY TOMATO TOFU AFTER MAHDUR JAFFREY

Instead of tofu, barely ripe bananas, cut into large chunks, may be added to this sauce, simmered until tender and garnished with fresh coriander. Serve alongside Curried Bananas with rice.

- 500 g firm tofu, squeezed and cut into 1-cm-thick slices
- 2 tablespoons oil
- 1 teaspoon fennel seeds
- ½ teaspoon black onion seeds (*kalonji*)
- 1 tin (410 g) whole peeled tomatoes, chopped
- 1 tablespoon ground coriander
- 1 level teaspoon ground turmeric
- 1 teaspoon grated fresh ginger
- 6 cloves garlic, crushed
- 1 teaspoon *sambal oelek* (minced chilli)
- ½ teaspoon salt

Heat oil in a large frying pan, add fennel seeds and *kalonji* and stir briefly. Add the tomatoes and the rest of the ingredients and stir through. Simmer until a thick sauce is formed. Put tofu slices into the pan with sauce and allow to heat through thoroughly. May be served at room temperature, a few hours later.

Sweet 'n' Sour Tofu Rissoles

Sauce

1 small onion, diced
1 green capsicum, diced
1 large carrot, diced
4 button mushrooms, diced
2 tablespoons oil
1 heaped teaspoon ground ginger
2 tablespoons light soya sauce
3 tablespoons cider vinegar
1 cup pineapple chunks
½ cup pineapple juice
2 teaspoons cornflour

Fry vegetables in oil until soft. Add ginger, soya sauce, vinegar and pineapple. Stir well. Mix cornflour with juice and add to vegetable mixture to thicken. Reserve to serve with rissoles.

Rissoles

400 g textured tofu
1 small onion
2 tablespoons soya sauce
2 teaspoons minced ginger
1 teaspoon minced garlic
2 cups soft breadcrumbs
(or 1 cup cooked rice)

Combine all ingredients in a food processor and blend well. Form into small ovals and bake in an oiled pan at 200°C for 12–15 minutes.

Bean Taco Mix

2 cups brown beans, cooked and left with a little water
2 medium carrots, chopped
1 medium onion, chopped
1 stick celery, chopped
1 tablespoon tomato paste
2 teaspoons paprika
2 teaspoons cumin
pinch of salt
a shake of white pepper

Simmer all ingredients until thickened.

Beans with Lemon and Oil

2 cups dry brown beans, soaked and cooked until tender

Dressing

4 tablespoons olive oil
3 tablespoons lemon juice
1 clove garlic, crushed
pinch of salt
ground black pepper
3 tablespoons chopped parsley
Lebanese bread, toasted, to serve

Stir dressing ingredients into warm beans and serve with toasted Lebanese bread.

Butter Beans with Cinnamon

Useful for any tinned or cooked beans.

2 cups butter beans, cooked
2 x 5 cm cinnamon sticks
2 tablespoons olive oil
1 large onion, sliced in wings
1 cup crushed tomatoes
1 teaspoon tomato paste
pinch of salt
ground black pepper
toast, to serve

Heat oil and brown cinnamon sticks. Add onion and fry lightly, then add beans, tomatoes and seasoning with a little of the bean water. Allow to simmer for about 15 minutes until well combined. Serve warm on toast.

Chickpea and Yoghurt Breakfast (Fatteh)

Loubna Haikal describes this as a heartwarming breakfast dish on a cold winter morning with friends. This recipe comes from Alaseel, one of my favourite Lebanese restaurants in Sydney.

2 cups chickpeas, cooked well and drained, reserving cooking water/stock
Lebanese bread, cut into small squares and fried in hot oil
1 cup Greek-style yoghurt
½ cup hot chickpea stock
½ teaspoon salt
1 clove garlic, crushed
2 tablespoons pine nuts, toasted
paprika
a little ghee, to garnish (or melted butter)

In each serving bowl, place 2 large tablespoons of drained, hot chickpeas and cover with fried Lebanese bread squares. Add garlic and salt to yoghurt with stock, beat well and pour over Lebanese bread. Top with pine nuts and a little paprika and ghee.

Chickpea and Pumpkin Patties

2 cups pumpkin, cooked and mashed
1 tin (410 g) chickpeas, drained
2 tablespoons green onion, chopped
4 tablespoons feta, crumbled
1 tablespoon fresh thyme, chopped
(or 1 teaspoon, dried)
salt
ground black pepper
2 tablespoons sesame seeds

Mash all ingredients except sesame seeds with a potato masher, form into golf ball size patties and flatten slightly. Roll in sesame seeds and bake on baking tray lined with baking paper at 200°C for 15 minutes.

Cottage Bake

The different layers of this dish make a bowl of lentils rather interesting.

1 cup brown lentils, soaked
2 bay leaves
sprig of savory
2 tablespoons olive oil
1 large onion, chopped
1 stick celery, chopped
6 medium mushrooms, quartered
3 cloves garlic, crushed
2 cups good tomato pasta sauce
with herbs
1 teaspoon of salt
ground black pepper
4 medium-size potatoes, boiled, peeled,
left to dry and coarsely grated
few leaves thyme
olive oil

Boil the lentils with bay leaves and savory until tender. Sauté onions, celery and mushrooms in oil with garlic and add to cooked lentils with salt and pepper. Pour everything into a deep casserole dish, cover with tomato sauce, potatoes over the top and sprinkle with a little thyme and olive oil. Bake at 200°C, until crisped.

Couscous for Hotpot

2 cups couscous
2 cups stock from boiled vegetables and chickpeas

Bring stock to the boil, add couscous and turn off heat. After 5 minutes, fluff the couscous to serve.

Relish

3 tablespoons olive oil
6 onions, sliced in wings
1 cup blanched almonds
1 teaspoon turmeric
2 teaspoons cinnamon
125 g raisins

Brown onions in oil on a high heat. Add spices and nuts, and finally raisins, stir thoroughly and serve at room temperature with the hotpot and couscous.

Chickpea Hotpot with Couscous and Relish

I love this as a one-pot meal in winter. Well, almost one-pot. The relish is outstanding and the couscous … mmm.

2 cups chickpeas, cooked
500 mL water from cooked chickpeas
2 teaspoons paprika
1 teaspoon cumin
6 cloves
500 g butternut, cut in large cubes (or carrots)
1 capsicum, quartered
2 turnips
1 swede
1 parsnip
4 stalks celery, cut in chunks
1 onion, quartered
a few green beans

Bring the chickpea water to the boil with paprika, cumin and cloves. Add all vegetables and boil for about 10 minutes, until tender. Add chickpeas.

Lentil Lasagne with Ricotta

375 g red lentils
3 bay leaves
2 tablespoons olive oil
1 large onion, finely chopped
2 medium carrots, diced
2 cloves garlic, crushed
1 medium eggplant, diced
1 vegetable stock cube
3 cups pulverised tomatoes
  (or pasta sauce)
300 g fresh ricotta cheese
ground black pepper
1 teaspoon oregano, dried
handful of fresh basil leaves, roughly torn
box (250 g) lasagne sheets
parmesan cheese, to dress
3 cups tomato purée, to dress
2 cups water, to dress

Boil lentils in water with bay leaves until tender. Meanwhile heat a little olive oil in a large saucepan and sauté onion and carrots for a few minutes. Add garlic, eggplant, crumbled stock cube and tomato pulp, then simmer until the eggplant is tender. Mix lentils in. Stir ricotta, pepper, oregano and basil through. Layer sauce with instant lasagne sheets, top with shredded parmesan. Mix the water with the tomato purée and pour over the top. Bake for about 45 minutes at 180°C.

Lentil Pottage on Toast

A delectable light meal in a hurry.

2 cups red lentils
2 bay leaves
1 vegetable stock cube
2 cloves garlic, crushed
1 tablespoon olive oil
capers, chopped, to garnish
parsley, chopped, to garnish
feta, crumbled, to garnish
black olives, halved, to garnish
Italian bread, to serve

Cover lentils and bay leaves with boiling water and cook for about 20 minutes, until tender. Add stock cube, garlic and oil and continue cooking, stirring from time to time until porridgey. Serve on thick wedges of toasted Italian bread, garnished with capers, parsley, feta and black olives.

Lentil Salad

4 cups brown or green lentils, cooked
2 medium tomatoes, chopped
4 shallots, sliced
1 Lebanese cucumber, diced
½ cup chopped mint
2 tablespoons black olives, halved
2 tablespoon olive oil
2 tablespoons lemon juice
1 level teaspoon salt
ground black pepper
croutons, to serve
yoghurt, to serve

Toss all ingredients with lentils and serve with croutons and a bowl of yoghurt.

Lentil Soup with Beans and Rice (Maklouta)

This is a mid-winter soup that will power you up on the coldest day.

1 cup brown lentils
1 cup chickpeas
½ cup brown beans
½ cup rice, uncooked
½ cup onion, chopped
1 cup carrot slices
1 teaspoon caraway seeds
3 tablespoons olive oil
1 teaspoon salt
good shake of white pepper

Soak the beans, peas and lentils overnight. Rinse and cook until tender. Sauté the onions and carrots lightly with the caraway and add to the soup pot with the rice. Add seasoning and boil for about 30 minutes.

Lentil and Spinach Soup (Shorba b'Addas)

Real Lebanese comfort food.

1 cup green or brown lentils, soaked overnight and well-cooked, until tender
6 cups water
½ cup onion, chopped
3 tablespoons olive oil
6 cups spinach, chopped (or 200 g frozen)
small bunch of coriander, chopped
1 teaspoon salt
shake of white pepper
80 mL (⅓ cup) lemon juice

Fry onion gently in oil, add all the ingredients, except for the lemon, to the lentils and simmer until the spinach is cooked. Add lemon juice and adjust seasoning.

Mixed Bean Soup

My cousin John, a great cook, described his mother's soup to me …

1 cup kidney beans, cooked
1 cup borlotti beans, cooked
1 cup small white haricot beans, cooked
2 bay leaves
small bunch of winter savory
1 medium onion, chopped
1 leek, chopped
1 turnip, chopped
3 medium carrots, chopped
3 sticks celery, chopped, with leaves
2 tablespoons tomato paste
salt
sprinkle of white pepper
big handful of parsley, chopped
few celery leaves, chopped
750 mL water (from cooking the beans, if possible)

Put beans and their cooking water into a large pot with bay leaves and savory and bring to a simmer. Add vegetables and simmer for about 30 minutes, until tender. Add the tomato paste, seasoning, parsley and celery leaves and boil for a further 15 minutes.

Mung Dhal

*For ten days after experiencing bereavement, Bengalis have to eat a mourner's diet that consists of plain dahl, vegetables and rice. This recipe is rather more spicy. Asafoetida (*hing*), dried powdered resin from the root of the giant fennel (a great digestive aid) can be found at Indian grocers. It is sometimes informally called garlic powder, as the Hare Krishnas use it instead of onions and garlic.*

2 cups split mung dhal (peeled, split mung beans)
5 cups water
1 teaspoon turmeric
2 teaspoons ground coriander
1 tablespoon ginger, grated
pinch of hot chilli
2 tablespoons oil
2 teaspoons cumin seeds
pinch of asafoetida
1 large onion, chopped
1 teaspoon salt
½ cup coriander, chopped

Wash mung dhal and add to a large saucepan with water, turmeric, coriander, ginger and chilli. Boil for about 1 hour, stirring occasionally until tender. Heat oil, sizzle seeds, add asafoetida and onion and sauté until shiny. Add to the dahl saucepan with salt and coriander. Boil up for a few minutes.

Lima Bean Loaf

2 cups lima beans, cooked
1 small onion
2 tablespoons snipped sage leaves
½ cup oats (or fresh brown breadcrumbs)
½ cup water from cooking the beans
2 bay leaves
1 tablespoon oil

Place all ingredients into a food processor and blend, adding bean water until a chunky batter forms. Place in an oiled loaf tin, decorate with bay leaves and oil and bake at 180°C for about 20 minutes.

Pea and Leek Soup with Lemongrass

1 cup split green peas
1 x 5 cm cinnamon stick
2 bay leaves
8 cloves
1 x 25 cm stick lemongrass, halved vertically and bruised
1 large leek, finely chopped
2 tablespoons oil
ground black pepper
1 teaspoon salt
1 tablespoon shredded fresh ginger
2 medium tomatoes, peeled and diced, seeds removed
1 tablespoon mild green chilli, deseeded, deveined and finely chopped
3 medium potatoes, peeled and diced
1 teaspoon lemon zest

Wash peas and cover with boiling water. Bring to the boil with cinnamon, bay leaves, cloves and lemongrass and simmer until the peas are almost tender. Meanwhile, sauté leek in oil until soft, add pepper and salt, ginger, tomatoes and chilli and reserve. Add potatoes to peas and simmer until cooked. Add leek and tomato mixture with zest and boil up. Set aside, preferably in wonder-cushion, and allow flavours to develop before serving.

Sprout Salad with Sesame

3 cups mixed sprouts
6 shallots, chopped
1 tablespoon olive oil
1 tablespoon soya sauce
4 tablespoons sesame seeds, toasted

Cover sprouts with boiling water and leave for 2 minutes before draining. Mix through the rest of the ingredients and top with the sesame seeds.

Red Lentil Soup with Spices and Tomato

A rich, warming meal served with yoghurt – no bread necessary.

4 tablespoons olive oil
2 medium onions, diced
1 bay leaf
½ teaspoon ground cumin
1 teaspoon sweet paprika
1 teaspoon turmeric, dried (or 1 tablespoon fresh, grated)
1 teaspoon garam masala
1 teaspoon ground ginger
ground black pepper
pinch of minced hot chilli
1 teaspoon minced garlic
2 cups red lentils
1 vegetable stock cube
6 cups boiling water (more later if desired)
1 tin (800 g) whole peeled tomatoes, chopped
4 medium carrots, sliced
1 tablespoon tomato paste
½ cup chopped coriander
½ cup chopped parsley
salt (optional)

Sauté onions lightly with bay leaves. Add spices, chilli and garlic and stir through. Add lentils, stock cube, water and the rest of the ingredients. Simmer until tender. Add salt if desired.

Spinach and Black-eyed Bean Bake

½ bunch of silverbeet, chopped, stalks included
2 cups cooked black-eyed beans
1 tablespoon olive oil
1 large onion, chopped
½ cup chopped coriander
½ cup chopped parsley
pinch of salt
pinch of white pepper
pinch of cinnamon
1 teaspoon pimento (allspice)
2 cups potato, diced
2 teaspoons tomato paste in ½ cup hot water (or bean stock)
yoghurt, to serve

Heat oil and fry onion lightly. Mix all ingredients, put into a covered casserole dish and bake at 190°C for about 35 minutes, until the potato is tender. Serve with yoghurt.

Cooked Bean Salad

1 tin (410 g) beans of choice, drained and rinsed (or 2 cups beans, cooked)
1 small, sweet onion, finely chopped
2 medium tomatoes, finely diced
1 tablespoon chopped parsley
ground black pepper
1 tablespoon lemon juice
2 tablespoons oil

Toss all ingredients with pepper, lemon juice and oil.

Lima Bean Salad

1 tin (410 g) lima beans (or 2 cups cooked lima beans)
2 tablespoons sun-dried tomatoes in oil, slivered
1 small cup roasted capsicum, cut in strips
1 clove garlic, crushed
ground black pepper
1 tablespoon balsamic vinegar

Mix all ingredients and allow to stand for a few minutes before serving.

Borlotti Bean Salad

1 tin (410 g) borlotti beans (or 2 cups borlotti or kidney beans, cooked)
2 medium tomatoes, finely diced
2 shallots, green and white parts, sliced
½ cup black olives, pitted
1 tablespoon mint, chopped
1 tablespoon lemon juice
1 tablespoon white wine vinegar
2 tablespoons oil
ground black pepper

Toss together.

Canellini Bean Salad

1 tin (410 g) canellini (or other cooked, small white beans)
1 large carrot, finely diced
1 green capsicum, cut in small dice
2 shallots, white and green parts, thinly sliced
2 tablespoons chopped parsley
2 tablespoons lemon juice
2 tablespoons oil

Toss together

Mixed Bean Salad

1 tin (410 g) three-bean mix
1 medium, red onion, finely chopped
1 teaspoon dried basil
1 tablespoon lemon juice
1 tablespoon cider vinegar
ground black pepper

Toss well and serve with garlic bread.

White Bean Salad

1 tin (410 g) butter beans
2 tablespoons basil pesto
1 tablespoon lemon juice
1 tablespoon balsamic vinegar

Mix well, stand for a short while and serve.

Crossing the bridges of understanding and
love, we arrive at our true home.

– Thich Nhat Hanh

Then and Now

In the 1950s and 60s, my father delighted in gigantic Chevrolets and we had family trips to visit uncles and aunts in the north, or shorter drives to bowling tournaments in nearby Queenstown or Butterworth. The car was packed with my parents, five children, one or two Boxer dogs and a nursemaid who sometimes slapped peace into scrapping children.

My father was a speed freak and my mother's anxiety became full-blown. On newly tarred roads he'd push the speedometer to one-hundred-and-ten miles an hour. The swaying, floating feeling led to expressive nausea in the back seat, which was efficiently dealt with by Johanna or Katrina.

My mother, Bertha, and Askim, in the garden of Antonville, my childhood home, 1959.

Feeding such a crowd called on all the ingenuity Cook could muster to pack a picnic that would fill and entertain us and not make us more carsick than usual. Yoghurt sandwiches were therefore a definite no-no, while the salty taste of Marmite was an antidote.

One of the longer trips we took was from East London to Kroonstad in 1963: we went to visit Uncle Victor, my father's older brother, and members of the extended Yazbek family who had remained in the Orange Free State. We set off early one winter morning in the June school holidays. It was still dark when my mother came to wake us. We slipped into our shorts and cardigans and carried our dreams into the car my father had already packed, cursing impatiently all the time. The basket of food for the trip (*zuwedie* in Arabic or *padkos* in Afrikaans), my mother's only weapon during fights or episodes of whining boredom, was secreted at her feet. Rosaries were patted in pockets and the Chev swung out of the driveway and up Devereux Avenue toward Cambridge and the road to Queenstown.

My mother listened to the news and weather forecast on the radio in case snow had closed mountain passes on the road north. All clear, she turned off the radio and the silence was filled with my father's droning Hail Marys and our responses. The best part of the prayers was grace – 'Bless us oh Lord …' and the tin of sandwiches was opened.

A cry went up from Anita as the boiled eggs dipped in salt were handed round. 'Pooh, what's that stink?'

Cucumber sandwiches were Lebanesed with olive paste, avocadoes from our garden were mashed with a vinaigrette dressing, strong cheddar from the Cradock dairy was crumbled onto brown bread with lettuce. Carrot sticks and tiny florets of parsley were the edible garnish.

Two-and-a-half hours later we pulled into Queenstown, my mother's birthplace, where her sister Phyllis and family still lived and ran The Waldorf Cafe on the main street. We unfolded ourselves from the car slowly and headed in to Uncle Joffre and Auntie Phyllis's arms. After the waitress had taken our order – yes, we still had space for toasted cheese and Coke – my father started to get agitated.

A proud car owner in East London, South Africa, 1937 – the Saffys still love cars.

'Come on, come on, we have a long drive ahead.'

The road over Pennhoek Pass took long sweeps ever upward as we left the Karroo Plains and climbed the escarpment to the north. My mother's replenished picnic hamper now contained oranges, guavas and crunchy red apples that my father tore into with gusto. Aliwal North on the banks of the Orange River was a regular motel stopover. I still remember the blue one we stayed in: the paint must have been cheap, as absolutely everything was painted blue – walls, ceilings, window frames. We always got back on the road straight after a breakfast of eggs and bacon, which was forbidden at home, but we left the blue place while we were still chewing.

No sooner were we in the car for the last leg when my mother would start.

'I wonder what Freda is making us for lunch.'

And my tactful father responded with, 'Yes, Victor and I were lucky to marry such good cooks.'

The only similarity between those long car trips as a family in South Africa and my trips today in Australia is the food I pack and the distance I drive; I am usually alone in the car. On my way from Sydney to Bangalow, as I cross the Hawkesbury at Mooney Mooney, I eat my first mandarin. After the wide, grey-green river, the bend of the road to the north tells me I am truly 'going away'. Tea-stop number one, beneath the pearly rock at Buhledelah, makes all the distractions and beauty of Sydney quite distant now. When I cross the Manning River at Taree, I feel as though I am on the homestretch – there may be 500 kilometres to go but these bridges take me ever onward and inward.

Solitary driving and stopping at will for a view, or to write something that silence has dislodged, is as gratifying as arriving in the arms of loving friends – the moment when the city and all cares of home have fallen away. Enfolded in green hills, close to a blue and white sea, I become friend to myself once more.

Crowdy Head Lighthouse, heading north on the Pacific Highway from Sydney.

A Year of Picnics Around Bangalow

Nature has always been my salve. When I moved to the north coast of New South Wales I felt very much at home in that lush natural environment, green as it is with banana and macadamia farms and what's left of the Big Scrub.

Although I grew some of my own vegetables and herbs, the markets were a delight for an enthusiastic cook: avocadoes, bananas, garlic, chillies, macadamia nuts, mangoes and sweet potatoes, to list a few, sent me scurrying into my kitchen in a fever of invention. These recipes are mostly the result of that abundance.

In the early days I traded food with stallholders. Near the entrance, I'd meet the avocado lady and swap a few boxes of vegetarian meals for a basket of ripe avocadoes. From there I shared some of my avocadoes, for handfuls of garlic and chilli. By the end of my first year in Bangalow, I'd had picnics in every season in many beautiful places.

During the seasonal whale migration, from June to September, the view from the Byron Bay lighthouse and surrounding headlands held me in awe, as those giants followed their instincts in the face of treacherous human hunters. In June the whales head north to calve in Hervey Bay. On their return journey in September after they've calved, mothers and their young head south, passing Byron headland with a playful exuberance that draws aahs from the quiet crowds.

A bibulous picnic by the sea in East London, South Africa – courting couples at play, 1930s.

Before the whales arrived, one late May, my friend Karin and I drove to Lions Lookout in Ocean Shores, from where we could see down to Ballina and almost up to Queensland. As it was cooler with a bit of a wind, we had Vegetable Koftas and mugs of Mulligatawny Soup from a saucepan in my wondercushion, as we sat waiting to spot the first whale.

Once the migration began in June, I took a picnic to Byron lighthouse. Breakfast was a Wintry Apple Compote and Pumpkin Scones with macadamia butter, followed by a lunch of Potato and Macadamia Curry Pies with Banana Sambal.

In the lighter months after July, my friend Merran, a nurse in Brisbane, came to visit me in Bangalow on many weekends. We swam and walked and talked and picnicked. She found Sark's *Eat Mangoes Naked* in the guest room and it became her bible. We had brunch at the top of the Coolamon Scenic Drive, with the view across Possum Shoot taking in the whole of Byron Bay and the Julian Rocks. We were fortified for the day with some Nut Pastry Rolls with a spicy tomato sauce, a few crudités and Macadamia Basil Pesto with avocado.

A pair of Sirens in the sand dunes in East London, South Africa, 1930s.

Later in the year, Merran celebrated a big birthday at my home, with her family and friends who booked into local bed and breakfasts. Unsure of the weather, I served a varied menu of hot and cold dishes, beginning with Macadamia and Pumpkin Soup and a bathful of chilled Avocado Soup. After setting up the buffet I retreated to my bedroom, where I swapped my apron for belly-dance regalia and flung my middle-aged torso almost into their plates. Fortunately, some of her friends were medical, as one gentleman's heart could barely take the strain! For the rest of the party, the guests were as lively as the food.

Early the next day, despite cloudy heads, the party continued: a few of us took the winding road through sweet green hills to the country market at the Channon. As we got out of the car, cow pats and herbal cigarettes tickled our nostrils. Circles of stalls with flags on top beckoned us onward. In open spaces, faded hippies reclined decorously on Indian cotton bedspreads. The pace made our hungover group look positively fresh.

Our baskets filled with avocadoes, nuts and fruit, to add to the Curry Muffins in the boot, we set off down Terania Creek Road to Protesters' Falls in Nightcap National Park, the site of the first eco-blockade that saved these forests, in 1979. It had been raining and as we climbed through the lush growth to the waterfall, vegetation smells and birdcalls enveloped us. We stood in the cool mist watching the rushing water. Back at the picnic site in the bosom of that old growth forest, we ate lunch quietly, thanking those who defended that place.

In December, my children came to stay for a few weeks. We walked on the breakwater at Brunswick Heads but the sea was wild so we drove across the bay to Wategoes. Under the trees, we fell into the picnic basket of boiled eggs, vegetables and a pot of Macadamia Satay Sauce kept warm in the wondercushion. Although it was a hot morning, fanned by a gentle sea breeze, we spent hours reading and nibbling.

The day my children left I couldn't stay alone in the empty house so I walked into Bangalow to the lower end of Station Street and the path that runs along Byron Creek. This last remnant of the Big Scrub rainforest, a tiny moist patch, right there in the village, is a haven of dark shade created by a canopy of tree branches. The ground is uneven with thick tree roots and boulders covered in green moss. Some said they saw platypus, but I never did. Almost at the end of the path, on a clearing, an old school desk stood, waiting for me, my notebook and pencil. My children had eaten the pantry bare; my picnic food that day was the thoughts and feelings that accompany change and farewells.

On grey winter mornings in Sydney, my mind flies once more to Bangalow and the markets, to whale watching and picnicking. Before too long, the suitcase comes out of the cupboard and I return to those people and places of sweet and delicious memory.

Lebanese youngsters in East London, South Africa, 1940 – were they matchmaking or just scouting for talent?

WINTRY APPLE COMPOTE

I use the best Stanthorpe apples from the farmers' markets in Bangalow.

3 large green apples, peeled and coarsely grated
2 medium bananas, diced
4 tablespoons raisins
1 x 5 cm cinnamon stick
2 cups orange juice

Stew on a low heat until it becomes a gluey pottage, ensuring it doesn't stick and burn. Serve at room temperature.

AVOCADO AND LIME SPREAD

2 ripe avocadoes, mashed
1 small tomato, finely diced
2 tablespoons finely snipped chives
2 tablespoons chopped coriander
2 tablespoons lime juice
salt
pepper

Blend all ingredients well and use as a spread or dip.

AVOCADO VINAIGRETTE

Hass are the creamiest, Reed are bright green and ball-shape, with a nutty flavour.

2 ripe avocadoes, mashed
1 tablespoon white wine vinegar
1 tablespoon olive oil
pinch of sugar
pinch of salt
pinch of black pepper

Mash all ingredients to a velvety paste.

Avocado with Tahini

Serve with crudités of, among others, cauliflower, carrot, celery and snow peas.

2 ripe avocadoes, mashed
½ teaspoon salt
1 clove garlic
3 tablespoons tahini
80 mL lemon juice
little water

Blend garlic and salt in a food processor, add tahini and lemon and, with the machine running, add about 80 mL water to thin the sauce. Add avocadoes to the processor bowl and run until a smooth, pale-green sauce results.

Avocado Soup

Serve with crisp fingers of Turkish toast.

Soup

3 medium, ripe avocados, peeled and pitted
1 cup vegetable stock, cooled
2 tablespoons sherry (or balsamic vinegar)
2 tablespoons lemon juice

Garnish

1 medium, red onion, finely chopped
150 mL yoghurt (or soft tofu)
½ cup leaf coriander, chopped
½ cup red capsicum, diced

Liquidise ingredients to form a thick sauce and pour into a large serving bowl, preferably glass. Garnish the top with colourful arrangements.

Choko Loaf

Delicious with a garlicky tzatziki and mixed-leaf salad with tomatoes.

1 medium potato, peeled and cut in 1 cm slices
3 medium chokoes, peeled and cut in 1 cm slices
1 medium grey zucchini, cut in 1 cm slices
2 small, red onions, peeled
2 tablespoons baby capers
1 teaspoon rosemary, dried
2 tablespoons parsley, chopped
black pepper
4 tablespoons crumbled feta
2 tablespoons grated parmesan, for top
6 eggs, beaten
lemon wedges, to serve

Steam all the vegetables until tender. Place the potato slices on the bottom of an oiled 23 cm oven dish, 10 cm deep. Cover with choko, chopped onion, capers, herbs, seasoning and feta. Finish with zucchini slices, sprinkle with parmesan, pour eggs over and bake at 190°C for 50–60 minutes, until set. Serve with lemon wedges.

Curry Muffins

A wonderful snack, using a leftover curry.

3 cups besan flour
½ teaspoon salt
3 teaspoons baking powder
3 tablespoons oil
3 large eggs, beaten
4 cups mixed vegetable curry (not too much sauce)
2 tablespoons chopped coriander

Mix flour, salt, baking powder, oil and eggs. Stir vegetables and coriander through. Bake in a muffin tray at 190°C for 20 minutes. Serve with a fruity chutney or Banana Sambal.

Egg Baked in a Tomato

A comforting supper when one is tired.

1 tennis-ball-size tomato
2 thin slices feta cheese
1 large egg
pinch of oregano, dried
pinch of pepper

Slice off the bottom of the tomato and scoop the insides into a small microwave bowl. Put the tomato on top, place a piece of the cheese in the bottom of the tomato, break the egg in, sprinkle with seasonings, top with remaining cheese and cover with sliced-off end. Microwave on high for 2–3 minutes, until the egg is cooked. Allow to cool for a few minutes.

Egg Baked with Spinach and Feta

A little snack at the beginning or end of the day.

2 tablespoons cooked spinach or chopped cooked mushrooms
1 tablespoon crumbled feta
1 egg lightly beaten

Mix all the ingredients and pour them into a ramekin. Microwave on high for 1–2 minutes until set, and serve inside a flat bread roll.

Banana Sambal

The Indian lady at the banana farm sometimes presented me with a whole box of ripe bananas, 'for cakey'. One day I gave her one of my banana cakes, but she wrinkled her nose and said, 'Is good for you; Indian people no like.'

4 ripe bananas, sliced
2 tablespoons mayonnaise
1 tablespoon fruit chutney
1 level teaspoon curry powder

Mix together well and serve immediately.

Macadamia Basil Pesto

1 packed cup, fresh basil leaves
small handful of parsley
3 tablespoons macadamia nut paste
pinch of ground pepper
2 tablespoons parmesan cheese
1 clove garlic, crushed
2 tablespoons olive oil
2 tablespoons lemon juice

Mix ingredients in a food processor to form a paste.

Macadamia Satay Sauce for Dipping

Serve with steamed vegetables, tofu or fresh rice paper rolls. Freezes well in small tubs for later use.

1 small onion, finely diced
1 tablespoon oil
1 tablespoon minced ginger
½ teaspoon minced hot chilli
1 cup macadamia butter
1 tablespoon lemon juice
1 tablespoon soya sauce
1 tablespoon rice or cider vinegar
1 tablespoon palm sugar (or brown sugar)
½ teaspoon tamarind concentrate in
  ½ cup hot water
pinch of salt
½ cup skim milk (or coconut milk)
extra ½ cup hot water, depending on
  desired consistency

Fry onion in oil until shiny, add ginger and chilli then the rest of the ingredients, except water, and stir to blend. Slowly add water until sauce is desired thickness.

Macadamia and Pumpkin Soup

750 g pumpkin, peeled and diced
1 cup macadamia butter
2 large onions, chopped
2 tablespoons oil
1 tablespoon grated ginger
pinch of hot chilli
1 clove garlic, crushed
1 large, white potato, peeled and diced
1 L vegetable stock
1 tin (400 g) whole peeled tomatoes
salt
1 cup chopped chives (or shallot tops)

Sweat onion in oil, add ginger, chilli, garlic, pumpkin and potato. Stir about, add stock and tomatoes and simmer for about 40 minutes, until all tender. Add macadamia butter and purée until smooth. Season with salt, and finish with chives or shallot tops.

Mulligatawny Soup

1 medium onion, diced
3 tablespoons oil
500 g pumpkin, diced (or carrot or sweet potato)
1 tablespoon fragrant curry powder
6 cups vegetable stock
1 tablespoon fruity chutney
½ cup cooked rice
2 tablespoons lemon juice
salt
minted yoghurt, to garnish

Sauté onion in oil until shiny. Add pumpkin and stir about for a minute with curry powder. Add stock and bring to the boil, then add chutney and simmer until everything is tender. Purée soup and return to heat. Add rice and lemon juice and test for salt. Serve hot with a little minted yoghurt in the middle.

Nut Pastry Rolls

2 sheets ready-rolled puff pastry
1 cup macadamias, finely chopped (or almonds)
2 slices wholemeal bread, crumbled
1 medium onion, grated
1 clove garlic, crushed
1 medium potato, boiled, peeled and mashed
2 teaspoons tomato paste
salt
pepper
spicy tomato relish

Blend ingredients, form into sausage shapes and wrap in puff pastry. Cut into 5 cm rolls, prick top and bake at 220°C for 15 minutes. Serve warm with Tomato Salsa with Cumin.

Potato and Macadamia Curry Pies

Sweet potatoes, cooked and roughly mashed, may be used instead.

2 sheets ready-rolled puff pastry
4 large potatoes, boiled, cooled, peeled and coarsely grated
1 cup macadamia pieces
1 large onion, peeled and finely chopped
1 tablespoon oil
1 teaspoon cumin seeds
2 teaspoons fragrant curry powder
1 vegetable stock cube, dissolved in 100 mL hot water
pinch of salt
pinch of pepper
Banana Sambal, to serve

Heat oil and fry onion until shiny. Add seeds and curry powder and stir about. Add the stock, mix well and add potato and nuts. Fork through until all coloured. Set aside to cool. Fill puff pastry – either as one large pie with top and bottom crust or 8 small pastie shapes, and bake at 220°C until browned. Serve with Banana Sambal.

Pumpkin Scones

These are wonderful with macadamia butter and ginger jam.

2 cups mashed pumpkin
300 g light sour cream
3–4 cups self-raising flour
up to 200 mL warm water

Bake diced pumpkin in a pan with a little water at 200°C for about half an hour – it gives a stronger flavour. Mix cream into mashed pumpkin and slowly work flour in with a knife, adding up to 200 mL warm water to form a soft scone dough, not a batter. Turn onto a floured board and cut into shapes. Pack closely together onto a baking tray lined with baking paper and bake at 220°C for about 18 minutes.

Rice Salad with Mango

I love this salad as a one-dish meal with boiled eggs.

Dressing

½ cup mayonnaise
1 tablespoon fruit chutney
2 teaspoons fragrant curry powder

Mix ingredients and reserve to dress warm rice.

Salad

2 cups rice, cooked
2 cups chopped ripe mango
4 medium tomatoes, chopped
1 medium Spanish onion, chopped
1 green capsicum, chopped
1 teaspoon fennel seeds, toasted
3 tablespoons sunflower seeds, toasted

Dress the warm rice and allow to cool. Stir the remaining ingredients through, top with mixed seeds and serve. This salad is best eaten all at once as the rice hardens in the fridge.

Sweet Potato Chips with Chat Masala

Indian-style spicy wedges.

1 kg yellow sweet potatoes (*kumera*), sliced into thick wedges
3 tablespoons chat masala
4 tablespoons olive oil
Yoghurt with *Accelerant*, to serve

Sprinkle chat masala and oil over wedges. Toss well and bake at 200°C for about 45 minutes. Serve with Yoghurt with *Accelerant*.

Vegetable Koftas

Great morsels for a picnic. Many vegetables work in this dish – for example, onions, pumpkin, fennel, zucchini and even choko. Serve with a good chutney, yoghurt and a salad of leaves.

6 cups mixed vegetables, coarsely shredded
1 teaspoon salt
small bunch of fresh coriander, chopped
1 tablespoon grated ginger
1 tablespoon ground cumin
1 tablespoon ground coriander
1 teaspoon black mustard seeds
1 teaspoon ground fenugreek
1 teaspoon ground turmeric
pinch of dried hot chilli flakes
125 mL oil
300 mL (more than 1 cup) besan flour

Sprinkle salt over vegetables and allow to stand for 30 minutes. Add the rest and blend all together well by hand, squeezing juice from vegetables. Slap into a mound in the mixing bowl and leave to rest briefly. Bake little mounds on a baking tray lined with baking paper at 200°C for about 18 minutes.

Pat's Tofu Dip Almost Humous

My neighbours in Bangalow knew I loved food and cooking and would sometimes bring me an unusual recipe that was particularly good. This is Pat's: I tasted it at a drinks party on their deck one late summer evening. It is lovely with seaweed rice crackers and crudités of fresh vegetables.

300 g silken tofu, drained
2 cloves garlic, crushed
2 tablespoons lemon juice
3 tablespoons tahini
1 tablespoon soya sauce
3 tablespoons yoghurt
few drops Tabasco sauce
black pepper

Blend all ingredients well.

Tomato Salsa with Cumin

1 tin (800 g) whole peeled tomatoes, finely milled
3 tablespoons tomato paste
pinch of salt
ground black pepper
pinch of hot chilli
1 teaspoon ground cumin
1 teaspoon sugar
1 medium red onion, chopped
1 teaspoon wine vinegar
1 tablespoon olive oil
2 tablespoons chopped parsley

Reduce tomatoes over a moderate heat. Stir in paste and boil for three minutes. Add remaining ingredients, seasoning to taste and allow to boil for a minute, then set aside to cool and serve hours later.

Tzatziki

Renee's Greek recipe – lovely with curries.

2 cups Greek-style yoghurt
3 Lebanese cucumbers, peeled, grated and left to drain for an hour
3 tablespoons *labne* (or drained yoghurt)
ground pepper
2 cloves garlic, crushed
1 tablespoon white wine vinegar
1 tablespoon olive oil

Blend all ingredients well and refrigerate.

Yoghurt with *Accelerant*

So called by my son, who has a low chilli threshold.

500 mL thick yoghurt
2 cloves garlic, peeled
1 tablespoon grated ginger
2 medium to hot green chillis
1 handful of mint leaves
small bunch of coriander
zest and juice of 1 lemon
pinch of salt

Place yoghurt in a bowl. Mix all other ingredients well in food processor and add to yoghurt. Use as a dipping sauce or side dish.

And when you crush an apple with your teeth, say to it in your heart, 'Your seeds shall live in my body, and the buds of your tomorrow shall blossom in my heart, and your fragrance shall be my breath, and together we shall rejoice through all the seasons.'

– Kahlil Gibran

My Foreign Heart's Home

Joe, my Lebanese carpenter, came over to tell me about the trip he would take in April – fly to Amman, bus to Jerusalem for a week, then back to Jordan and fly in to Beirut for a lengthy stay.

'Come with,' he cajoled, 'it will be good to see Jesus places – I never *bin zere*,' and this religious man, like Scheherezade telling the stories of the Arabian Nights, launched himself into telling me 1001 saints' stories.

Somewhere, in the middle of his religious drone, I heard mention of '*ze* best *Libaneez* cake shop in Sydney'. That grabbed my attention and, as he left to go to church, I began to plan my annual *mafroukie* feast. *Mafroukie* is a cake that looks as if it accidentally fell out of the tin: semolina fried in ghee, smothered in clotted cream, heavily studded with toasted almonds and pine nuts, bathed in syrup with a dab of crushed pistachios and rose petal jam on top. Now you know why I eat it only once a year. In my 20 years here, I have eaten it in Dulwich Hill, Lidcombe, Newtown, Lakemba, Granville and Kogarah. Now I'm off to taste it in Merrylands.

On a bench at Strathfield station, I wait next to a friendly Sri Lankan lady who asks me where I'm from.

'Hornsby,' I say, but I know that where she lives, everybody is from somewhere else, so I continue, 'South Africa, but my origin is Lebanese.' The Indian woman and girl on the other side of me shuffle and I feel their sideways looks. I wonder whether they had to leave Uganda, South Africa or somewhere else. My questions are flung aside by a smiling Chinese father who swings his little girl up and down to her elated cries of 'whee!' before the train to Merrylands pulls in.

At the station kiosk, the Lebanese proprietor happily directs me '*zis* way and *zat*', to Heart to Heart, the bakery I'm looking for. The streets are lined with shops that grab my nose and I find myself salivating: Sitari, the Afghan spice shop, Kabul, the grocer, Turkish All Goods, Indian Spice Emporium, Asian and Chinese mixed business, all selling ingredients for adventurous eaters and cooks. But I must keep moving, as the mercury is rising. Suddenly the aroma of *mnaish b'zaater* (Lebanese thyme pizza) coming from the pizzeria makes me stop to look at haloumi and spinach pies, and I hear a young man with a big gold watch say to his mate, over Cokes and pizzas, 'The Gold Coast is great – such good value, and the women are gorgeous.'

The people on the street match the shops, including an old man, shirtless on the footpath, tucking into a pie doused in red. Passing a shopping mall, loud with familiar chain stores, I catch sight of a neon heart sign. Aah, my cake shop. I fall into its air-conditioned cool. Giant wedding cakes, crowned with cathedrals or smothered in sugar roses, fill a cabinet alongside hundreds of equally decorated Lebanese chocolates, which, in density, make Lindt feel like snowflakes on the tongue.

A lady with thick black eye make-up and bottle-brass hair approaches. 'I'll have a *mafroukie* and an English Breakfast tea, please.'

'How you know *zis* name?'

'*Mafroukie*, the cake of my childhood. My granny made it for us until my mother said it was too unhealthy and she had to stop.'

'You not *Libaneez*, you don't look *Libaneez*.'

I smile, 'I am.'

'You *arr willcum*. Nice to meet you.'

How reminiscent of my first experience twenty years ago, a few weeks into my arrival in Sydney. In Campsie, a man in a bakery window was rolling dough and spreading it with olive oil and thyme. I inhaled the aroma of my grandmother's kitchen.

Granny Isabel visiting old Beirut with her sister and husband (Amin Habs) and children, 1956.

Noticing my excitement, he asked, 'You *Libaneez*? Where you from?' And to my reply, he said, 'My home, your home, you *willcum* anytime.' I left his shop with pizza and a lump in my throat. This was a man from a war zone, who'd made his home here and opened his hospitable Lebanese heart to me, a very privileged newcomer from South Africa.

The generosity of Middle Eastern people humbles me because their life experiences are remote from mine. They populated Beirut, the coast of Jounieh and orchards of the Bekaa Valley in war, occupation and peace. Although I cannot identify as one of those who have suffered, they welcome me as part of the shared gene pool. Some of the prejudice against them today reminds me of what my ancestors encountered when they first went to South Africa.

In my search for the familiar, people sometimes tell me I don't look like what I'm claiming. 'You are Spanish,' they mostly say. What does it matter, I think to myself. My place is in my heart, where my personal history hangs, sometimes light, sometimes heavy.

As I wander back to the station, trying to get home before the heat is too much, I think of the railway lines of Sydney as arteries carrying lifeblood to all extremities. The train opposite me is going further south-west to Cabramatta, home of the largest Vietnamese temple and also the smallest Laotian temple, with its big-hearted community. Here delis and markets, side by side, sell South East Asian and Eastern European delights.

Going back I sit on the left of the carriage. A lady opposite me opens a Collins book, 'Afghanistan' in big letters across the cover. Pencil poised, she moves her lips over each syllable. I admire her faceted gold earrings. Is she on her way to language classes? The Taliban won't reach her body here. All the Afghans I've met speak of their country with brimming eyes.

Behind her, two tall, well-groomed men sit together. I think of Kurds, my mind among Saddam's ruins and the decimated minorities of his tyranny. So many here, from so many places, are trying with dignity to move into the future beyond the brutality of their history. The history of this country reached a place, in 2008, of 'saying sorry' to the Aborigines.

As the train moves, I see an Orthodox basilica on my right and soon after, on my left, the impressive Gallipoli mosque at Auburn. Here in Australia, we are nest building; we create shrines to our beliefs, our ancestral systems. Our comfort food abounds. No one can say we don't belong. *Mafroukie* and my search for it waken the tastebuds of memory and carry me to distant reaches of my city, a place where I find myself feeling mostly at home.

Family Favourite Sweets

My mother and father were both health fanatics and dessert was always fresh fruit. In fact, there are only a couple of recipes here that my mother made regularly (once a year!): Christmas cake, Christmas Pudding and Speculaas Biscuits.

We were brought up on wholemeal bread, brown sugar (if any) and quantities of fresh fruit and vegetables. Even though two of her brothers were doctors, my mother had a mistrust of the medical profession, and believed that 'a good diet, exercise and making friends' would cure anything. Sometimes though, she'd visit Mr Hofstee, the herbalist at the market. She even led Auntie Eileen astray: one afternoon, Auntie, whose husband, Albert, was an anaesthetist, called my mother into the pantry to show her a familiar brown bag with Mr Hofstee's label on the front. Replacing it behind the huge flour bin, Auntie put her finger to her lips and whispered, 'Don't tell Albert.' I wondered why ever not, after all, my father also took herbs sometimes.

My mother occasionally made something as decadent as fudge or a chocolate slice. It could have been for my birthday party when I turned seven in 1960. Judy, my best friend from kindergarten, with whom I am still in regular contact, was at my party with twenty or so other friends from school. She still tells me how embarrassed she was when her parents forgot to collect her once the party was over. I was long bathed and put to bed, with poor Judy standing next to my bed when the mellifluous tones of her mother's voice calling '*Tsoody, Tsoody*' floated from the front door, down the long hall and into my bedroom.

The Bangalow fruit flan is a way of using up tired fruit salad. It turned out so well the first time I made it that Michael and Pete, who were helping me in my garden that day, thought, when I offered them each a slice, that I meant they should leave only *one* slice from the entire twelve-serve flan.

In East London, Billie Mulholland's husband played hockey with my father in the 1940s and 50s, and she gave my mother her special Christmas cake recipe. Every year my mother drew up a list of who would be getting one of her cakes: the nuns at the Mater Dei Hospital, the convent where we went to school, the Brothers at de la Salle College, Mrs Boltman, who did our sewing and alterations; the list was long and caused my father to weep at all those cakes being given away. He loved warm fruitcake, but Mother insisted that the cakes were stored and brandied over a period of weeks before being eaten. Sometimes he stole into the pantry and helped himself, but my mother's ensuing fury made it barely worth it.

Because we had an Esse coal stove with four ovens as well as an electric stove, the baking was over in no time: pantry shelves groaned and a brandy fug hung in the hot kitchen during those humid November days.

My mother was a young housewife, skilled in Lebanese cooking. Baking was only for special occasions. But my teenage interests in the kitchen were not always healthy, and she loved me to use my baking skills for her cake stalls. On one such baking day, an aunt walked into our kitchen and announced loudly, 'I'll have the flops.'

My mother, confident of my prowess, swung around, clicking her tongue. 'There aren't any, and there won't be any.'

She subscribed to the view that what we take in should be life-sustaining, to which I add that a decadent treat can be life-enhancing at the right time!

My parents at play – my mother always at the piano, my open-hearted father, a born entertainer, whose repertoire consisted, sadly, of eating worms and, happily, exuberant Afrikaans songs and a whole carnival from the American songbook.

Almond and Orange Slice without Egg

Not really a panforte, but so delicious.

- 1½ cups plain flour
- ½ cup cocoa
- 1 rounded teaspoon cinnamon
- 4 cups whole almonds
- 2 cups (or more, to taste) chunky orange marmalade (or other citrus), slightly warmed
- 1 or 2 dried figs, sliced (or 3 tablespoons candied ginger, chopped)

Mix all ingredients well, until they form a very stiff mixture. Spoon into a 2-cm-deep lamington tin lined with baking paper and bake at 180°C for about 20 minutes. Cool on a rack. Cover thickly on all sides with icing sugar, wrap in cling wrap and store. Keeps for about 6 weeks or may be frozen. Serve in thin slices.

Bertha's Speculaas Biscuits

My mother got this recipe for these traditional Dutch biscuits in the 1940s from an old Afrikaans woman in South Africa.

- 1 kg plain flour
- 500 g butter
- 1 teaspoon ground cloves
- 1 tablespoon cinnamon
- 1 tablespoon mixed spice
- pinch of salt
- 700 g raw sugar
- 1½ cups almonds, chopped (or your favourite nut)
- 1 dessertspoon bi-carb
- 200 mL port wine (or sherry or ginger wine)
- 2 eggs, beaten

In a large bowl, mix the butter with the flour until it forms a crumbly mixture. Add the spices, sugar and nuts. Add the bi-carb to the wine and eggs, then pour into a hollow in the dry ingredients. Mix well and form into a smooth dough. Leave this in a cool place or refrigerate for 1 hour. Roll out thinly and cut into shapes or bake scored, thin sheets of the dough on baking trays lined with baking paper at 180°C for about 20 minutes, until browned. Allow to crisp on the pan before removing to tins.

BANGALOW FRUIT SALAD FLAN

A lovely morning or afternoon tea treat in summer.

Crumbly Crust

- 4 tablespoons flour
- 1 tablespoon sugar
- 3 tablespoons macadamia oil
- 2 tablespoons macadamia nut pieces

Mix oil, flour and sugar until they form a crumbly mixture. Add nut pieces and press the mixture into a 23 cm pie dish. Bake at 190°C for about 15 minutes.

Filling

Use a leftover fruit salad that might contain mango, banana, pineapple, any stone fruit, berries, grapes, passionfruit, kiwi, apple or pear, all cut into small pieces. Melon and pawpaw become sloppy and citrus is too acidic.

- 1 cup milk (soya or coconut milk are also good)
- 1 teaspoon butter (not with coconut milk)
- 3 tablespoons sugar
- 3 cups leftover fruit salad and any juices
- 2 rounded tablespoons custard powder mixed with a little of the milk
- cinnamon, to sprinkle on top

Bring milk, butter and sugar to the boil, drop fruit salad in, heat through quickly, thicken with the custard powder paste and pour all into the baked crust. Sprinkle with cinnamon and return to the oven for about 10 minutes. Serve chilled.

Brandy Tart (Brandewijn Tert)

Tart

250 g dates, chopped
1 teaspoon bi-carb
180 mL hot water
¾ cup sugar
1 egg, beaten
2 tablespoons butter
1 tablespoon honey
1teaspoon vanilla
½ cup milk
1¼ cups self-raising flour
½ cup walnuts or pecans (optional)

Soak the dates in the bi-carb and water for 30 minutes. Mix the sugar, egg, butter and honey, add the vanilla, milk and self-raising flour. Add the date mixture and stir through. At this point, the walnuts or pecans may be added. Bake at 190°C in a large casserole dish for 30 minutes.

Syrup

1 cup sugar
180 mL water
1 teaspoon vanilla essence
1 tablespoon butter
½ cup brandy

Bring sugar and water to the boil, add the vanilla and butter, remove from the heat and add the brandy. Pour over tart as it comes from the oven.

Japie's Favourite Citrus Delicious (Japie se Gunsteling)

A self-saucing citrus pudding to remind us of Japie, whoever he might be.

2 eggs, separated
1 cup sugar
1 cup milk
¼ cup flour
1 cup orange juice
1 dessertspoon lemon juice
1 orange rind, grated
1 tablespoon butter, melted

Beat the egg yolks and sugar. Stir in the milk and flour. Add the juice, rind and butter and beat to mix. Fold in the stiffly beaten egg whites. Bake in a 23-cm buttered pie dish at 170°C, for 45 minutes.

BUTTER FLAKE PASTRY

125 g hard butter, diced
125 mL boiling water
up to 2 cups self-raising flour

In a large mixing bowl, melt the butter by pouring over the hot water. Stand for about 5 minutes. Using a broad-bladed knife, blend flour into the butter and water with a cutting motion and stir to combine, taking up as much of the flour as needed. Refrigerate for about an hour. Scrape out onto a floured board, roll out, sprinkle with flour, fold and roll again, then roll thinly and use for nut rolls, curry pies or sweet tarts. Bake at about 220°C, until browning.

CHOCOLATE FUDGE SLICE

This slice makes good a bad purchase or a failed recipe – put unwanted cake or biscuits into the food processor and use the crumbs to make this slice.

2 tablespoons butter
3 tablespoons castor sugar
4 tablespoons cocoa
4 cups crumbled fruitcake (or biscuits)
2 tablespoons chopped glacè ginger
(or dates or raisins)
1 egg, beaten
2 tablespoons brandy
nuts, to decorate
cherries, to decorate

Melt the butter and sugar, add the cocoa, then add the cake crumbs, fruit, egg and brandy. Stir well over low heat for about 8 minutes. Pack into a flat baking tray lined with baking paper, about 1 cm deep, and decorate the top with nuts or cherries. Refrigerate until firm. Cut into squares to serve.

Mrs Mulholland's Christmas Cake

For this recipe you will need konfyt, *which is obtainable from Asian grocers. You can use chunky melon jam instead.*

250 g butter
1 cup sugar
4 eggs
3 cups flour, sifted
¼ teaspoon salt
1 teaspoon cinnamon
1 teaspoon mixed spice
½ teaspoon nutmeg
¼ teaspoon bi-carb
200 g currants
200 g sultanas
125 g dates
125 g glazed pineapple
125 g *konfyt* (glazed paddy melon)
125 g glacé cherries
125 g nuts, chopped
½ cup brandy

Cream butter very well. Add the sugar and beat until white and fluffy. Add the eggs one by one. Mix in the flour, salt, bi-carb and spices. Stir in the fruit and almost all of the brandy. Prepare a 23-cm-round pan with baking paper. Bake at 140°C for 3 hours. When the cake has cooled, take it out of the oven and sprinkle with brandy.

Christmas Pudding

Mrs Slade's recipe book was my mother's baking bible. This recipe was prepared in October and hung in the pantry to dry for Christmas. As a child, I was always on hand at those marathon cooking sessions: scrubbed to the shoulder, I plunged my arms into the mixture to blend the ingredients. Cook then lifted the heavy bowl and scooped the batter onto the washed cloths, tied them up and put them to boil in the giant turkey pot. This recipe makes two large puddings.

3 cups flour
250 g butter
3 cups stale breadcrumbs
1 cup carrot, grated
375 g sugar
1 teaspoon cinnamon
1 teaspoon nutmeg
1 teaspoon mace
1 teaspoon salt
4–6 eggs, beaten
1 cup honey
1 teaspoon bi-carb
½ cup brandy
500 g seeded raisins
500 g currants
100 g glacé cherries
250 g candied citrus peel
2 cups good quality dates, pitted, for topping
brandy custard, to serve

Mix the flour, butter, crumbs, carrot, sugar and spices. Add the eggs and honey to the flour mixture. Then mix the bi-carb with the brandy and fruit (except dates), add this to the flour mixture, and pour everything into two 1.5-litre greased pudding bowls. Cover each well with pitted dates and top with foil, then boil for 3–4 hours. Store for a couple of weeks or freeze. To serve, thaw for about 8 hours and re-heat in the microwave.

Frozen Christmas Pudding

Use a log, ring, round or square container to produce a shape of your choice.

4 L plain vanilla ice cream, softened
4 tablespoons glacé ginger, chopped
6 tablespoons macadamia pieces
2 cups plain or Ginger Biscuits, crumbled
½ cup brandy (or a little less Cointreau)
2 cups plumped fruits (for example, raisins, sultanas, cranberries)
½ cup boiling water
grated dark chocolate, to decorate

To plump the fruits, put them into a microwave bowl with half a cup of water and boil for a minute. Set aside. Mix all the ingredients, line the container with cling wrap, fill with ice cream mixture, cover and freeze. Unmould by standing *briefly* in a sink of warm water. Invert, lift off the container and cling wrap and cover with grated dark chocolate.

Date Loaf

When Granny Isabel went to visit Uncle Henry in Welkom, someone gave her this recipe and evermore, she baked a loaf on Fridays and brought it over to us for afternoon tea.

1 cup dates, chopped
1 cup boiling water
¾ cup sugar
1 teaspoon bi-carb
2 tablespoons olive oil
2 cups flour, sifted
1 teaspoon baking powder
1 egg, beaten

Pour the boiling water over the sugar, dates, bi-carb and oil, then leave to cool. Add the flour, baking power and egg, mix, then bake in a loaf tin at 180°C for 40 minutes, or until a knife inserted comes out clean.

Ginger Biscuits (Gemmerkoekies)

3 cups self-raising flour
2 teaspoons ground ginger
3 tablespoons finely chopped glacé ginger
1 cup raw sugar
125 g butter
3 tablespoons honey
1 teaspoon bi-carb
2 eggs, beaten

Mix the flour, gingers and sugar. Bring the butter and honey to the boil, add bi-carb and stir into dry ingredients. Then add the eggs. Mix well. Shape into balls and flatten with fingers onto a baking tray lined with baking paper. Bake for 15 minutes at 180°C. Allow to harden in the cooling oven, if desired.

Passionfruit Tart (Grenadilla Tert)

Tert means 'tart' in Afrikaans, and also bears the English pejorative! So the judge who mistranslated 'pie', described the accused as a man who had a finger in every 'tart'.

½ cup grenadilla (passionfruit) pulp
nut of butter
½ cup sugar
2 eggs, separated
½ cup flour
1½ cups milk
pinch of salt
1 teaspoon baking powder

Beat the butter, sugar and egg yolks. Add the flour and milk. Add stiffly beaten egg whites with salt, pulp and baking powder. Bake at 170°C, for about 40 minutes in a 20-cm round tin.

Ice Cream with Halva

2 L softened vanilla ice cream
250 g pistachio *halva*, mashed

Blend *halva* into ice cream and re-freeze in a shape of choice.

Ice Cream from the Farm (Smitsrivier Roomys)

As teenagers we had to perfect our Afrikaans language skills in order to gain a university entrance pass. For this, we were sent to the taal *(language) farm, where we had lessons every morning and tennis or bushwalks in the afternoons – all in Afrikaans, of course. This delicious ice cream was an incentive to obey the language requirement: if we defaulted to English, we missed out on dessert that night.*

4 egg whites, beaten until stiff
1 tin condensed milk
1 cup cream, beaten until stiff
1 cup milk
1 teaspoon vanilla

Add the condensed milk to the egg whites and cream. Add the milk and vanilla and beat well. Pour into dishes, freeze, and beat again before completely set.

Malva Pudding (Malva Poeding)

Apparently there is a history of high cholesterol in some Afrikaaner families: perhaps it is because of their predilection for this pudding!

1 cup sugar
2 eggs
1 tablespoon apricot jam
1 cup flour
1 teaspoon bi-carb
2 teaspoons butter
1 teaspoon cider vinegar
almost half cup milk

Beat sugar and eggs till light and add jam. Sift the flour and bi-carb. Melt the butter with the vinegar and add to the eggs with the flour and milk. Beat well. Bake in a 20 x 30 cm dish at 180°C for about 40 minutes.

Sauce

200 mL cream
100 g butter
160 mL sugar
100 mL hot water

Melt all the sauce ingredients and pour over the hot pudding as it comes from the oven. Serve warm.

Macadamia Fudge

1 cup full cream milk
1 tablespoon butter
1 cup raw sugar
1½ cups macadamia nut spread

Melt all ingredients over medium heat and stir constantly for about 20 minutes until it pulls away from the sides of the saucepan into a ball. Scrape onto a tin lined with baking paper and spread to about 2 cm thick. As it begins to cool and firm, score into squares.

Koeksusters

These are Mrs de Witt's authentic Afrikaans sugar-packed treats. Mrs de Witt lived across the road from us when we were growing up. She did sewing alterations for all of us and was delighted to know when we were off to the farm to learn Afrikaans. 'That is amazing,' she said, 'Dis nou 'n wonder that you are learning our language.' Afrikaans was only recognised as a language in 1925 – until then it was forbidden to teach it.

Syrup

6 cups sugar
3 cups water
½ teaspoon cream of tartar

Boil ingredients for 5–7 minutes, then chill for 24 hours.

Dough

6 cups flour
3 heaped teaspoons baking powder
125 g butter
1–2 cups milk

Rub the butter into dry ingredients. Blend with enough milk to form a dough and knead well. Rest briefly. Form into 1-cm-thick ropes. Plait into 10 cm lengths and deep-fry. Drop into icy syrup for 2 minutes, drain and leave at room temperature.

Lemon and Lime Cordial

If limes aren't available, simply use lemons.

juice of 4 large lemons, zest thinly sliced
juice of 4 large limes, zest thinly sliced
4 large cups sugar
4 large cups water
1 teaspoon cream of tartar
1 teaspoon tartaric acid
1 teaspoon Epsom salts

Dissolve the sugar in the water and boil for 3–4 minutes. Add the zest, juice and salts to the hot syrup. Leave to stand for 24 hours, strain and bottle. Serve diluted, one-part cordial to ten-parts water, either hot or chilled.

Rice and Milk Dessert (M'hallabeeyee)

My petite mother, Bertha, used to love making this dessert, and as she ate it – at breakfast, lunch and dinnertime, with leftovers for the next day, she'd say gleefully, 'Ooh, I can feel myself getting fat!'

½ cup rice, finely ground
1 L milk
2 teaspoons orange flower water
2 teaspoons rose water
80 g sugar
blanched almonds, to decorate
pistachios, ground, to decorate

Wet the rice with half a cup of the milk. Heat the remainder of the milk and as it comes to the boil, pour in the rice and keep stirring until the mixture thickens. Add the sugar and simmer, stirring until the rice is completely soft. Remove from the heat and add the flower waters, then pour into a shallow bowl to chill thoroughly. Decorate the top with blanched almonds and ground pistachios.

MILK TART (MELK TERT)

Makes two medium tarts or one very large tart.

Shortcrust

125 g butter
2 tablespoons oil
1 egg
2 tablespoons sugar
2 cups flour
2 teaspoons baking powder

Cream together butter, oil, egg and sugar. Add the flour and baking powder and pull together to make a soft pastry. Press into a tart dish, prick all over and bake blind at 170°C for about 20 minutes, until browning.

Filling

500 mL milk
1 teaspoon butter
6 tablespoons sugar
1 heaped tablespoon flour
1 heaped tablespoon cornflour
4 eggs, separated
cinnamon, to decorate

Bring about three quarters of the milk to the boil, and all of the butter and sugar. Mix the flour and the cornflour with the rest of the milk, add yolks and beat slightly. Pour slowly into the boiling milk and stir until thick. Fold in the well-beaten whites and fill the just-baked pastry shell. Sprinkle the top liberally with ground cinnamon. Leave to cool at room temperature and serve.

Rusks (Egte Boeretroos)

Rusks are dried buns, or scones, dunked in coffee – genuine farmer's comfort. Rusk recipes vary in richness and complexity – I have used this one for years, as it mimics those richer, yeasted favourites of yore.

1 kg self-raising flour
1 cup raw sugar
2 teaspoons baking powder
good pinch of salt
250 g butter
2 eggs, beaten
1½ cups skim milk

Rub the butter into the dry ingredients and add the milk and eggs. Knead very slightly to bind. You may need a few more shakes of flour if the dough is too sticky. Pack the dough into a baking pan about 35 x 25 cm, and 5 cm deep, and score the top into fingers. Bake at 200° C for about 10 minutes, turning temp to 180°C for a further 30 minutes. Remove the tray from the oven and cover with a damp cloth for about 10 minutes. Remove the rusks from the pan, break into finger shapes and dry in the oven at 100°C for about 4 hours. Store in an airtight container for up to 2 months. Sometimes I bake all the dough and then, before drying, freeze half. In a few months time, break up the dough and dry the rest as needed.

Sago Soup (Boeboer)

Boeboer *is consumed by Malay Muslims in South Africa on the fifteenth night (halfway through) of Ramadan, the holy month of fasting.*

1 cup sago
about 3 cups water
3 x 3 cm cinnamon sticks
2 level teaspoons cardamom seeds
1 L full cream milk
handful of broken vermicelli
2 teaspoons butter
1 cup raisins
1 cup sugar

Boil the sago in water until it starts to become transparent. Add the cinnamon sticks and cardamom seeds. Keep simmering and stirring. Slowly add the milk, up to one litre. The mixture should be very runny, or else the next day it will be like cement. When almost done, fry the vermicelli in the butter. Add this to the pot with the raisins and sugar. Stir to prevent sticking and allow to stand. Serve warm or chilled.

Vegetable and Date Steamed Pudding

1 cup grated raw potatoes
1 cup grated raw carrots
1 cup chopped dates
1 cup flour
1 cup sugar
1 dessertspoon mixed spice
1 tablespoon jam
1 tablespoon oil
2 eggs, well beaten
1 teaspoon bi-carb (mixed with a little water)
ice cream, to serve (or custard)

Mix all the dry ingredients together, except the bi-carb, add the potatoes, carrots, dates, jam and oil. Mix well. Add eggs, then the bi-carb and mix again. Pour the mixture into a greased bowl and cover well with pierced foil. Steam for 2 hours and 30 minutes in a saucepan of water, taking care that it doesn't boil dry. Serve with ice cream or custard. Freezes well.

Self-saucing Chocolate Fudge Pudding

Do not try to turn this out of the dish. You will have a chocolate crust at the top and a thick fudge sauce at the bottom.

Batter

1 cup flour
2 teaspoons baking powder
½ teaspoon salt
⅔ cup sugar
1 heaped tablespoon cocoa
1 heaped tablespoon butter, melted (or 1 tablespoon macadamia oil)
½ cup milk
1 teaspoon vanilla essence
½ cup walnuts, chopped (or pecans)

Sift together the dry ingredients. Combine the butter, milk and essence, add to the dry ingredients and beat until smooth. Stir in the nuts and spread in a buttered, 6-cup casserole dish.

Topping

1 cup brown sugar
3 tablespoons cocoa
1½ cups boiling water
ice cream, to serve (or cream)

Mix the sugar and cocoa and sprinkle over the batter. Pour the water over, bake at 180°C for 50 minutes and serve with ice cream or cream.

Sweet Wheat Berry Dessert

In the Middle East, this dessert celebrates the birth of a baby – anise seeds for lactating mothers, walnuts for longevity, roses, the fragrance of love.

2 cups whole wheat berries, boiled
1 teaspoon anise seeds
2 tablespoons raw sugar
½ cup fresh walnuts
1 tablespoon rose water
3 tablespoons plumped raisins

While the wheat is still warm, stir through the rest of the ingredients and serve when cooled.

Sweet Potato Chocolate Cake

Grandma Buhagier, my auntie Susie's Maltese mother-in-law, made this cake for my father when he did some legal work for her. I was passionate about it and would sneak into the kitchen long after everyone had gone to bed to snaffle a piece from the fridge. She called it a Maltese Christmas cake, but I have asked every Maltese I've ever met in Australia and not one of them knows of this cake.

Cake

1 kg white sweet potatoes
1 cup sugar
1 teaspoon vanilla
2 tablespoons brandy
7 large eggs, separated

Bake the sweet potatoes in their jackets at 200°C, until soft, about 1 hour. Peel and purée. Mix the potato purée, sugar, brandy and vanilla. Add the egg yolks one at a time, beating well each time. Add stiffly beaten eggs whites. Bake in 2 x 20 cm cake pans at 180°C, for about 30 minutes. Cool completely.

Icing

2 tablespoons butter
2 cups icing sugar
½ cup cocoa
4 tablespoons brandy

Cream all together, decorate the cooled cake and refrigerate to chill thoroughly.

Nuts, seeds, pulses and purslane,

all good food for a good mood.

But remember, when all looks like

manure, get out there and plant

those roses!

Bits and Pieces

Suggested Menus

Menus should be coherent and should suit the occasion. Ensure that one's guests are either adventurous diners or in some way familiar with what you intend to serve.

Ingredients should not be repeated in different dishes – don't serve a tomato salad with a lasagne baked in tomato sauce, or a salad containing roasted pumpkin with pumpkin *kibbe*.

Try to mix colours on a plate: a selection of dips like *humous* or *babbaganouje* (both pale) with a spicy tomato salsa, Black Olive Tapenade, a ruby beetroot or a golden carrot dip.

When serving vegetarian meals to a growing family, try to ensure a good protein component – eggs, yoghurt, tofu, legumes or nuts in any one-pot meal. Dessert, if not too sugary, can sometimes complement the nutritional value of a meal.

Mezze is Lebanese *antipasti*, like Spanish *tapas* or Chinese *yum cha* – hundreds of little bowls with all sorts of different flavours, usually at room temperature, characterised by plenty. Use any of the recipes in Chapter 1 and some of the salads in Chapter 4.

Use your imagination and fresh or dried herbs to spice up legume salads. Or simply add a handful of cooked or canned beans to your favourite tossed salad when you're in a hurry.

Toasted seeds and nuts add a crunchy alternative texture: try pepitas, sunflower seeds, sesame seeds, blanched almonds, walnuts or shelled pistachios. Finely chopped radish and turnips, and matchsticks of carrot and beetroot, are also good for crunch. Try different sprouted grains and seeds (mung, alfalfa, lentil, onion, snow pea) for fresh variety.

On the topic of breakfast, nutritionists and health professionals have rules about this meal. In my experience, across many different cultures, only personal preference rules apply. Some prefer a sweet, light breakfast, like Europeans who enjoy a pastry. Others eat plenty of fresh fruit, sometimes adding yoghurt and nuts. And some insist on muesli or porridge. Some will eat anything savoury, such as risotto or leftover pasta. Rice and curry is especially favoured by some Indians and Sri Lankans. My daughter eats *humous*, olives and cucumber with *labne*, a typical Middle Eastern breakfast. The bottom line for me is: make it low GI with some protein, and whatever takes your fancy.

Home

Home Alone

Egg Baked in a Tomato
Egg Baked with Spinach and Feta

Family Lunch

Macadamia Satay Sauce
Steamed vegetables, boiled eggs and tofu
Plain rice
Chocolate Fudge Slice

Family Dinner

Cottage Bake
Tomato Salad with Purslane
Wintry Apple Compote

Entertaining

Winter Lebanese Dinner

Mains

Lentil and Spinach Soup

Za'ater Crisps

Eggplant Casserole with Nuts

Green Salad with Haloumi Cheese

Okra Relish

Sweets

Japie's Favourite Citrus Delicious – warm

Winter South African-style Dinner

Mains

Mulligatawny Soup with yoghurt

Bobotie with Nuts

Yellow Rice with Raisins

Sweet Potato Chips with Chat Masala

Salad of finely diced cucumber and tomato

Sweets

Warm Brandy Tart with cream or ice cream

Entertaining

Easy Summer Lunch

Mains

Avocado Soup

Loula's Eggplant Omelette

Boiled baby potatoes

Mixed Salad Leaves with Pomegranate Molasses Dressing

Sweets

Milk Tart

Summer Lebanese Feast

Mains

Plate of olives and pickles

Broad Bean Dip

Chilli Refresher

Spinach Galette

Silverbeet Stalks in Tahini Sauce

Cauliflower with Lemon

Kibbe of Red Lentils

Eggplant Roulade

Lebanese Breads

Sweets

Ice Cream with Halva

Entertaining

Summery Mediterranean Lunch

Mains

Chickpea and Pumpkin Patties
Auntie's Pine Nut Sauce with Garlic
Stuffed Tomatoes
Eggplant Patties
Lima Bean Loaf

Sweets

Fresh fruit and ice cream

A Wake

Zucchini Bites
Bite-sized squares of Labne Pie
Roasted almonds or pumpkin seeds
Pumpkin Scones with jam
Date Loaf
Ginger Biscuits

Entertaining

Cocktail Snacks

Assorted olives and nuts
Nut Pastry Rolls with a spicy tomato salsa
Pat's Tofu Dip
Carrot Dip with Dill Seed
Walnut Spread
Vegetable crudités
Labne-stuffed Mushrooms
Corn and Artichoke Fritters
Almond and Orange Slice without Egg

A Mezze Table

Bowls of olives and soaked or salted nuts
As many dips as your table can hold – Labne in olive oil, Beetroot Dip, Babbaganouje, Carrot Dip with Dill Seed, Roasted Red Capsicum Dip, Walnut Spread
Lebanese breads or toasted Turkish fingers
Green Beans with Caramelised Onion
Cauliflower with Lemon
Lentil and Rice Paté (M'jadra)
Okra Relish
Rolled Vine Leaves or Stuffed Zucchini or Stuffed Tomatoes or all
Any kind of kibbe – ball or loaf

Salads

Salads for a South African-style Lunch

Rice Salad with Mango
Curried Bean Salad
Saucy Bean salad
Onions in Mustard Sauce
Tofu Salad with Cabbage and Cashews

Salads for a Mediterranean Lunch

Almost Niçoise Salad
Any legume salad
Farmer's Salad (*Fatousch*)
Beetroot with Tahini
Cabbage Salad with Lemon
Kebabs of Tofu

Picnics

An Early Winter Lunch

Vegetable Koftas and Yoghurt with *Accelerant*
Mulligatawny Soup
Fresh fruit

A Whale-watching Breakfast

Wintry Apple Compote
Pumpkin Scones with macadamia butter and apricot jam
Potato and Macadamia Curry Pies
Banana Sambal
Pat's Tofu Dip and crudités

August Brunch

Nut Pastry Rolls with a spicy tomato salsa
Avocado and Lime Spread with crudités

Spring Lunch for a Crowd

Crudités
Chickpeas with Tahini
Harissa with Beetroot
Chilled Avocado Soup
Mushroom Patties with Dipping Sauce
Warm Choko Loaf with Tzatziki
Breads and cheeses

Picnics

Forest Picnic After the Party

Avocado Vinaigrette
Curry Muffins
Corn Pudding

December Seaside Picnic

Open Vegetable Pies
Macadamia Satay Sauce with boiled eggs and vegetable crudités
Fresh fruit

Healthy Vegetarians

And some information for parents of sudden vegos

A food is not necessarily essential just because your child hates it.

– Katherine Whitehorn

Children need to eat more than three meals a day: they need four to five good feeds per day, in quantity to suit their age, size and appetite. Excessive roughage in the diet can speed up the digestion and inhibit the absorption of nutrients from the intestines. For example, zinc is absorbed from the large bowel. A diet containing too much insoluble fibre, three cups of unprocessed wheat bran in one day, for example, and this goes for adults as well, can prevent the absorption of zinc and cause the symptoms of nutritional deficiency.

Children living in a vegetarian household, living normal active lives, should be neither under- nor overweight. As they get older and they are not suffering from any known food allergy, they should be encouraged to eat a wide range of fresh and dried fruits, vegetables, nuts, grains, legumes and seeds. Over-indulging in sugar or processed carbohydrate (white flours and pastries) can dull the appetite for health-giving foods.

Preservatives, colours and flavourings should be avoided at all costs.

Bean and lentil sprouts are a good source of calcium, amino acids and proteins, and older children can be shown how to make their own using a jam jar with holes in the lid. Put in two tablespoons of washed lentils or mung beans. Soak in water overnight. The next day, drain and store in a dark place, rinsing twice a day until the sprouts have grown enough to be eaten. Keep in the fridge for up to three days.

If energy levels are flagging or concentration is poor, check their diet to ensure that sufficient iron and protein are being consumed on a daily basis. And if in any doubt, always be sure to get good professional advice.

It is a good idea to include a variety of grains and seeds in the diet as their various nutritional values add protein and minerals; they are also useful in reducing too much reliance on wheat.

Low-fat skim milk, low-fat yoghurt, ricotta, cottage and yellow cheese are all good sources of protein and calcium. However, take care with too much yellow cheese: this can clog the system and be too fatty. As well as protein, free-range eggs add iron and B12, while mushrooms, seaweed and possibly legume sprouts also add some vitamin B12. Too much reliance on animal products can reduce our intake of plant foods; as well, mindful of the difficulties some people have with dairy products, this guide, inspired by Rosemary Stanton's *Eating for Peak Performance*, focuses on nutrients derived from non-animal sources.

Iron

Iron deficiency can make one tired and listless. Baked beans, cereals, dried fruits, green leafy vegetables, legumes and nuts are all good sources of iron. The yeast in wholemeal bread destroys phytic acid, which ordinarily binds iron in whole grains and makes it unavailable for absorption. Sourdough bread, lacking yeast, can block full iron absorption. Oxalic acid binds the iron in spinach. Red grape juice, on the other hand, is a good source, because the grapes are crushed with the seeds, which are high in iron. Tinned apricots are also said to contain some iron. Additionally, combining a meal with a serve of fresh fruit or vegetables, which contain vitamin C, increases the absorption of iron. For example, eating a mixed salad with a kidney bean dish is good, or try *tabbouleh*, a whole grain mixed with salad ingredients and lots of lemon juice! Finally, the tannin in strong tea inhibits iron absorption, so it should not be drunk with a meal.

Calcium

Aside from dairy products, nuts (mainly almonds) are a good source of calcium. As well, fruit and vegetables such as broccoli, cabbage and oranges are helpful. Baked beans are great but need to be mashed for small children.

Soya products such as soya milk and tofu (soya bean curd) are particularly useful – tofu has seven times the calcium as the same quantity of cottage cheese.

Carob, that chocolate look-alike without the propensity to cause migraine, is full of calcium. The same goes for tahini made from unhulled sesame seeds.

Protein

Good quality protein is readily available from chickpeas, lentils, all beans (kidney, lima, borlotti, cannellini and soya) and peas, including peanut, also a legume. Eating sunflower, sesame and chia seeds increases the available nutritional variety. Nuts, as well as protein, add good oils to the diet. Pure nut butters, such as almond, macadamia, walnut or pistachio, are available from the supermarket. They are delicious on steamed vegetables, or, as a snack, just on a wholegrain cracker.

Soya bean products like soya milk and tofu (soya bean curd) can be used in different ways to increase one's protein intake.

Combining a cereal and legume (as in wholemeal bread and baked beans, or peanut butter on wholemeal bread) makes a great protein snack or light meal. In peasant cultures, traditional combinations like corn and beans or corn and sour milk sustain people doing quite heavy manual work.

Stir-fried vegetables with fresh soya beans (as *edamame*, in the freezer department) to which tofu or nuts are added, is a nutritious meal.

Tabbouleh a whole grain with vegetables provides protein and iron: the vitamin C from the tomato and lemon juice enhances the iron uptake.

Seeds

My mother always had jars of toasted seeds on the breakfast table – sesame, sunflower and hulled pumpkin that she sprinkled liberally on her toast with *labne* and tomatoes.

Sesame seeds, especially unhulled, are very rich in calcium – they need to be milled lightly or else they just pass through the digestive system; ground to a paste, they become tahini. Sunflower seeds contain polyunsaturated oil and a number of important minerals and vitamins. Pumpkin seeds are a good source of protein, zinc, and other minerals. Chia seeds are another new product from the Ord River irrigation scheme: used by the Aztecs, they have been found to be rich in omega-3, dietary fibre and protein with an anti-oxidant effect. They are great sprinkled on cereals.

Store all seeds in glass containers in the fridge and only toast a few at a time for immediate consumption. Sunflower, pumpkin and sesame seeds can be toasted in a dry pan over a medium heat until lightly browned. Cool and store for a day or two in a jam jar.

Nuts

The most commonly used nuts in Lebanese cooking and sweets are almonds, cashew, pine, pistachio and walnuts.

Nuts all contain protein and, especially walnuts and almonds, are a great source of omega-3 fats. As well, almonds contain phyto-oestrogen and are rich in calcium. Brazil nuts contain selenium, the new mood tonic. Peanuts, although high in protein, are not true nuts – they are actually legumes.

The best macadamias come from the north coast of New South Wales – at the markets buy them whole or in pieces, roasted, flavoured or, my favourite, macadamia nut spread – pure nut paste.

Dr Ross Walker, cardiologist and author of a number of books, including *What's Cookin' Doc?* recommends that we eat at least three nut-based meals a week. As with most recommendations, see what suits you.

When I was growing up, we had pecan nut trees next to the olive trees – they all bore profusely: stale pecans and walnuts can be bitter, even rancid, and can make you ill. I keep all nuts in glass containers in the fridge.

Why be a Vegetarian?

I am a vegetarian purely on humanitarian and mystical grounds; and I have never killed a flea or a mouse vindictively or without remorse.

– George Bernard Shaw

Country life as a committed vegetarian and animal rights supporter is challenging: I was distressed by frequent encounters with truckloads of animals on their way to the slaughterhouse.

Cane toads, however, were something else. They were introduced to control the cane beetle, but they have no natural predator, so they multiplied, destroying the balance of native fauna – the red-bellied black snake dies after eating the toxic cane toad, leading to a big increase in the brown snake population.

My dog's encounter with the toad's toxin drove me to drastic action: I'd step into the garden at night, don Wellington boots, lift a sharpened shovel over my shoulder and say loudly, 'I am so sorry,' and bring the weapon down with as much force as I could muster.

To kill or not to kill – or to let someone else kill for you … the vexed question. Not everyone has to be vegetarian: I'd never tell a Kalahari Bushman to stop hunting. He has been doing it humanely for hundreds of thousands of years, and it is an essential part of his diet and traditional ritual. The Bushmen have a whole spirituality built around the hunting and sharing of an animal, and they never take more than they can use at any one time – a sustainability that has been almost wiped out by contact with consumer-oriented Western society. There are many other traditional peasant cuisines that sustain a physically demanding lifestyle on a mostly grain and vegetable diet.

Today, our way of farming animals is cruel. They are confined against their natural instincts, filled with drugs and chemicals to stimulate growth and then trucked en masse to their deaths in slaughterhouses. Or, even worse, transported in the holds of huge ships to be ritually slaughtered elsewhere. Their cries touch all and their fear is tangible. The adrenaline produced in this process is deposited in the meat.

To my mind, this is mass murder, and it is not surprising that we become ill eating food produced with such suffering.

The environmental consequences of this type of farming are well known. Crops grown to feed animals instead of people cause unnecessary food shortages. Too many resources go into producing a kilo of steak for an affluent diner, while thousands starve daily all over the world. In conscience, in South Africa, I could not teach mothers how to make soya milk for their families using raw beans and fuelless cooking, and at my home serve a fillet of something that cost the equivalent of a poor person's food for a month. There is enough variety in the plant kingdom for us to be well-nourished and filled with vitality.

Vandana Shiva, in an article for *Resurgence* called 'Food is Everything', brings attention to the new battle we face in our greed for fuel:

> And when food is no longer the sacred web that connects us to the Earth and the cosmos, but a mere commodity, it can be transformed into biofuel to run cars while people starve. Hunger is an expression of a violent and unjust world, a world out of balance.

For Heather who works hard for animal rights in South Africa and for others working in poorer places where animals and humans suffer together, I offer you these thoughts.

According to Australian Vegetarian Society, vegetarians: have less food poisoning, less cancer, less heart disease; each save more than 1500 animals from being killed in a lifetime; save many litres of fossil fuel that would be used in a year to raise, transport, slaughter and process meat animals; have a smaller carbon footprint than meat-eaters; each feed seven starving people with the grains and beans that would be fed to one animal killed for a meat eater – a child dies from malnutrition every 2.3 seconds; indirectly prevent desertification of arable land from over-stocking and reduce the destruction of rainforests for cattle grazing.

I hope that after you have tried some of the dishes, you are seduced by the spices and exciting flavours, prepared using the bounty of the earth that we are so generously gifted with in Australia.

The Wondercushion

A wondercushion is two large bags or cushions loosely filled with small polystyrene beads, modelled on the hay boxes used in England during the Second World War: the principle is insulation. I first came across it in South Africa during the 1960s. Compassion, a church-run relief organisation that was working with the poorest of the poor, attempting to alleviate starvation, was encouraging people to use soya beans to increase their protein intake, but the preparation of one packet could use the whole month's fuel (kerosene) allowance. The wondercushion saves energy and time, and is an environmentally sound, healthy way of cooking. Best of all, nothing can get burnt.

As a vegetarian, I use a lot of legumes but have always used a wondercushion. It will soon be four years since I first installed a large (normal size) gas bottle to power my cooktop. The gas company keeps on sending me tempting offers to reorder from them: I think they imagine I have taken my custom elsewhere. Indeed I have not. The truth is, my original gas bottle is still powering my cooking.

Preparation

Generally, bring your almost full saucepan to the boil, heat through thoroughly, take it off the heat and nestle the pot in the bottom cushion. Cover this with the top cushion and leave to sit for up to eight hours.

Soups and casseroles – still raw, yet thoroughly heated through by boiling for about 10 minutes – can be put in the cushion at 9 am and will be ready and hot enough to eat at 5 pm.

Oats, corn or semolina porridge can be made at bedtime, simply by bringing the pot to the boil and putting it into the cushion. The next morning, there will be hot porridge for breakfast.

Never use a wondercushion on the floor. Place it in a solid basket or a firm cardboard carton and, when in use, ensure it is located on a bench top or well out of reach of pets and toddlers.

Prevent cats from lying on top of the warm cushion: they could unseat the cushion, along with the lid of the saucepan, leaving you with a caterole instead of a casserole.

I have a large wondercushion in the boot of my car, and I place any frozen or chilled purchases in there until I reach home. A wondercushion is also great at a picnic: in winter, use it to transport a pot of thick soup; in summer, a tub of ice cream.

COOKING

PASTA

Bring 1 litre of water to the boil with a little salt. Add 250 grams of pasta and as soon as it boils, remove from heat and nestle in cushion. Allow to stand for 30 minutes, then drain and serve. As pasta shapes vary, try out the times to achieve the texture you prefer.

RICE

Wash 1 cup basmati rice and add to saucepan with one and a quarter cups boiling water. Bring to the boil on the stove, remove from heat and nestle in cushion. Ready to serve after one hour; or may be left as long as necessary. It will remain warm.

LEGUMES

Put previously soaked beans into a saucepan. Cover amply with water and bring to the boil. Boil for about seven minutes, remove from heat and nestle in cushion for two hours. Soya beans and chickpeas take three hours. When removing cooked beans from cushion stir thoroughly, reheat, add salt and boil for a minute or two.

If you're in a hurry and have forgotten to pre-soak beans/chickpeas/lentils, put the required quantity in a saucepan, cover with boiling water, bring to the boil and cook for five minutes. Leave to rest covered for one hour. Rinse thoroughly and using fresh water, bring back to the boil and boil for 10 minutes. Nestle in the cushion and leave the beans and chickpeas for three to four hours, and lentils for one to two.

Making a Wondercushion

Join the four top pieces together, leaving a small seam for filling. Join the four bottom pieces together, leaving a small seam for filling. Use 60–70 per cent of a 30-litre bag of polystyrene beads (bean-bag filling), fill the bottom (bigger) cushion. Use the rest for the top (smaller) cushion.

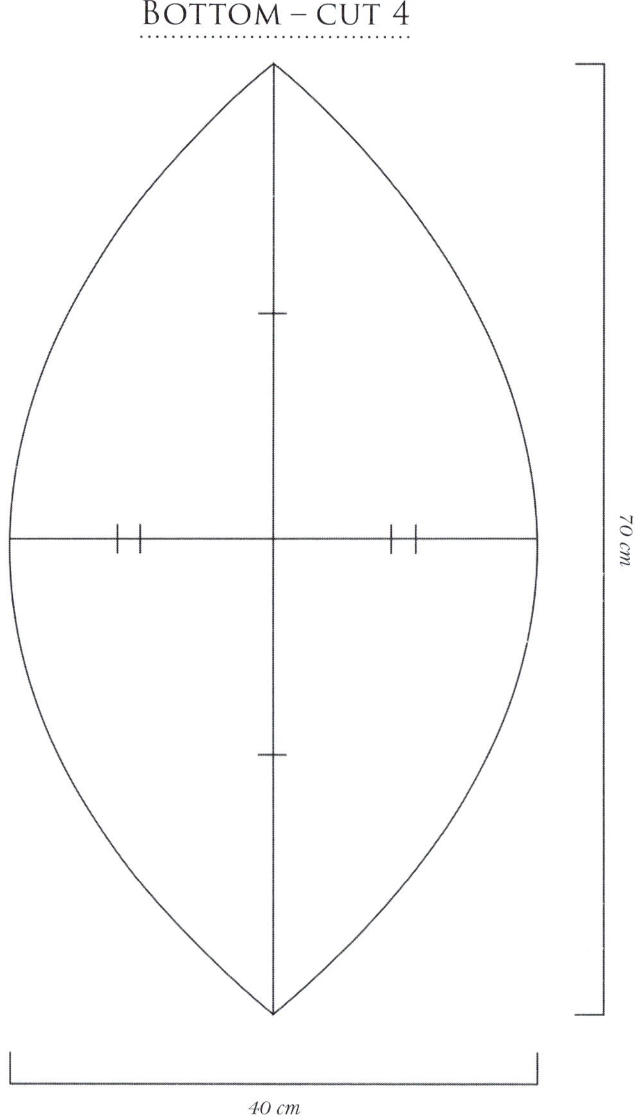

TOP – CUT 4

16.5 cm
22 cm
16.5 cm
36 cm
Bottom
Top
16.5 cm
22 cm
16.5 cm
70 cm
36 cm
40 cm

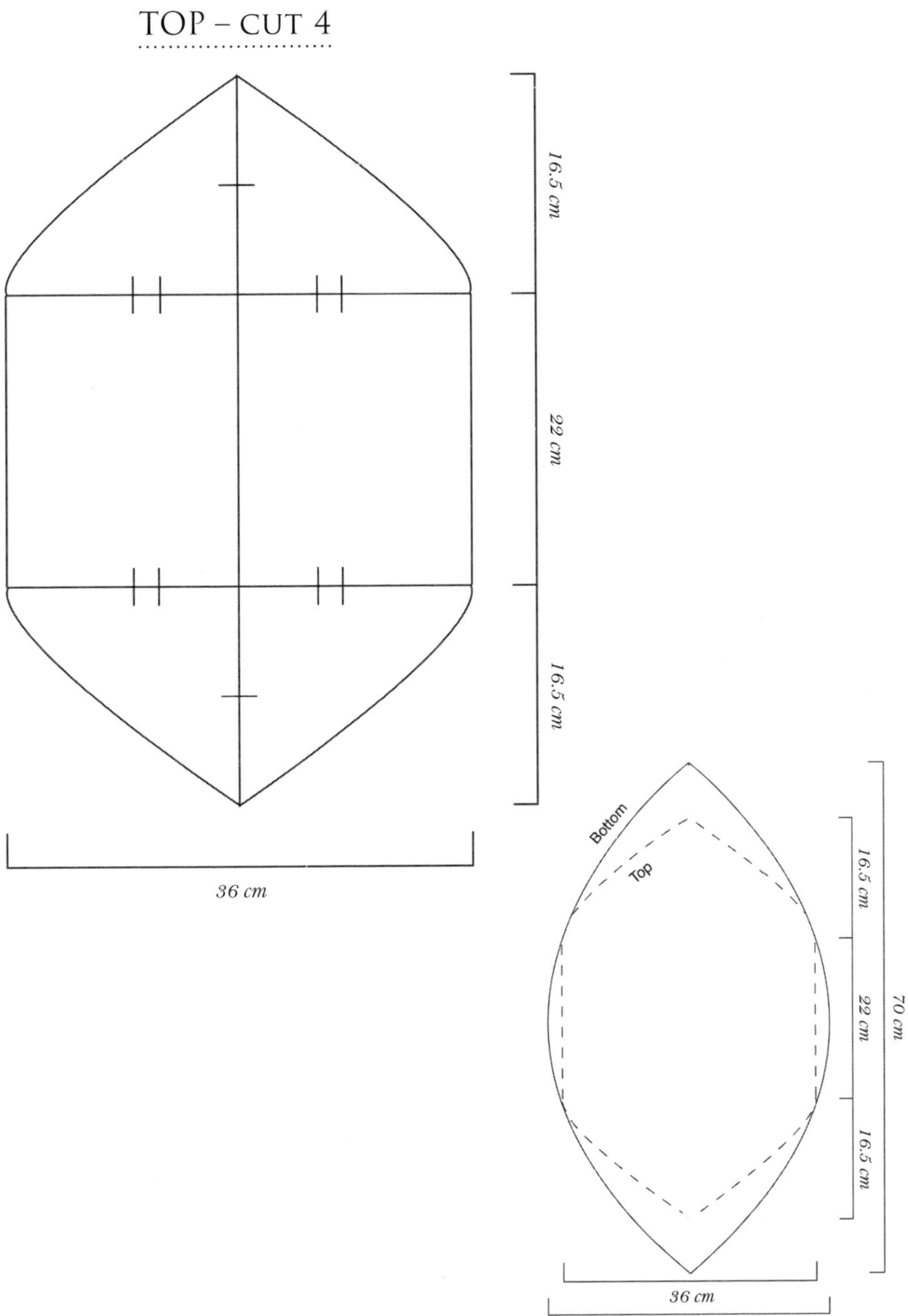

Waste Not, Want Not

When I was a child, my mother told us that leaving lights on in empty rooms could kill the men who sat peddling all day long at the power station to make electricity for us – they could die of exhaustion. When boiling water, store the leftovers in a flask for cooking or rinsing dishes and the efforts of those pedalling men will go a whole lot further!

When I first arrived in Australia from South Africa, I was shocked to see the amount of wasted food in garbage bins around the city. In my cooking school, I watched as a lightly blemished tomato was rejected, three layers of an onion were peeled and thrown away, and five centimetres of the pointy end of a carrot went into the bin. One of my hobby topics in class was over-consumption, overuse, overspending and throwing away.

There are many ways to avoid wastage. For example, when peeling a carrot or potato, use a peeler designed for the purpose: very few of us can use a knife without taking too much off. Best of all, though, if the vegetable is homegrown or organic, simply scrub it in cold water. My freezer saves me from wasting even a slice of onion.

No matter what, apply the goldfish rule: after three days, the water needs to be changed or the fish will get sick. Always keep everything covered in the fridge and, if reheating, heat thoroughly. When in doubt, compost!

Here are some tips for freezing all sorts of food, not forgetting the bags of sweated onion, carrot and celery mixture from Welcome to my Kitchen.

Burghul

When I buy a bag of *burghul*, if I am not going to use it all in a few weeks, I soak it in water for about an hour to reconstitute, squeeze it well, then bag and freeze it in two-cup amounts. Old *burghul* has a rancid smell, ruins a dish, and can cause heartburn.

Celery

A whole head is often too much for immediate use. Wash and use what will be eaten raw, then dice the rest and sweat it in a large microwave bowl on high for a few minutes, depending on the quantity, with a dash of olive oil. Bag and freeze it in one-cup amounts for later use in stews, muffins, soups and pasta sauces.

Coriander

Fresh leaf coriander doesn't keep well – wash what remains from your recipe, shake dry, chop roughly and freeze for later use in soups or curries.

Fennel

Slice thickly in rings, heat a little olive oil in a saucepan and, when smoking, drop the fennel in, then cover and simmer for about 20 minutes. Finish with lemon juice, grated zest, salt and pepper. Freeze one-cup amounts for later use in soups, curries and sauces.

Mushrooms

When mushrooms are plentiful, I put four or five cups of button mushrooms in a covered microwave dish and cook them on high for five minutes. Leave to cool, pour off the liquid for use in a stock or sauce, or even add to salad dressings; freeze the mushrooms in small bags for later use in stews, curries or tossed into a tray of ready-roasted vegetables. They will be flavoursome as well as chewy – even tough enough for the carnivore longing for something to bite.

Oil

If you really want to fry something, use a medium-size wok, as it requires less oil than a frying pan, and discard the oil after use. I never use reheated oil.

Onions

If onions are plentiful, peel, dice and fry them in olive oil until shiny, then bag and freeze them in two-tablespoon amounts. If you have the oven on already, roast whole smaller onions in their skins for about an hour at 200°C, peel and quarter, then freeze for use in quiches, onion soup and salads. This saves a lot of time: when a recipe calls for one chopped onion fried in oil, I grab a little bag from my freezer.

Pumpkin

Peel and cut into ten-centimetre wedges, then bag and freeze raw for later roasting or boiling. Roast small pieces of pumpkin, then bag and freeze. Carrots and sweet potatoes can also be roasted and frozen for use later in dips, soups and mashes.

Tomato Paste

Buy a large jar, freeze spoonfuls in an ice cube tray; pop out and store in a plastic bag in the freezer to grab when needed.

Acknowledgements

This food is the product of the whole universe,
the Earth and the sky and much hard work.
May we live in a way as to be worthy to receive.

– Thich Nhat Hanh's grace

Some of my favourite cooks and writers of Middle Eastern food are Paula Wolfert, Tess Mallos and Claudia Roden. Arto de Haroutounian does interesting things with a great variety of vegetables.

The first real Lebanese cookbook I owned was Rayess' *Art of Lebanese Cooking*, published by Librairie du Liban in 1966, which was mailed to me by a Beiruti cousin when I was just thirteen.

Mahdur Jaffrey is a wonderful Indian cook, whose books gave me confidence, early on, especially in working with spices. In Sydney, Ajoy Joshi's cooking classes are informative, delicious and very entertaining.

Full acknowledgements and gratitude to my children Stephen and Amelia, my students, and all my friends and their intrepid tastebuds.

Enormous thanks are due to my writing colleague, Susan Beinart, for her help over years with all my writing and her patience with my 'comma dyslexia'. Much appreciation is due to my editor, Ryan Paine at Wakefield Press: his great skill, forbearance and enthusiasm for this book sustained me through the process. The Bangalow Writers' Group encouraged me: their fundraising lunch held in my home started my experimentation with local produce.

Many thanks to Marguerite Dale for her wondercushion pattern.

In assembling this collection I remember with deep affection, my ever-present grandmother, my mother's mother, Isabel Haddad. She had gone to South Africa from Lebanon with her husband, my grandfather, Alexander, in 1910. Lebanese are great emigrants and they have taken their food and recipes all over the world. I have cousins in New York, Toronto, Buenos Aires, Johannesburg, Auckland, Sydney, Beirut …

As well, I am indebted to my Taiwanese, Sri Lankan, Jewish and Pakistani friends – indeed, to all my friends who let me peep into their kitchens.

C

D

E

F

M

N

Q

R

S

Wakefield Press is an independent publishing and distribution company based in Adelaide, South Australia. We love good stories and publish beautiful books. To see our full range of titles, please visit our website at www.wakefieldpress.com.au.